Solway is an imprint of
Paternoster Publishing, P O Box 300, Carlisle, Cumbria, CA3 0QS, UK

http://www.paternoster-publishing.com

05 04 03 02 01 99   7 6 5 4 3 2 1

**British Library
Cataloguing in Publication Data**

A catalogue record for this book is available from the British Library

ISBN 1-900507-77-3

Cover photograph: *Hale-Bopp Comet, April 1997,*
by Tricia Porter
Title page photograph: *Decoration in the Chapel, St Beuno's, North Wales,*
by Tricia Porter

Design and typesetting by David Porter
Printed in Great Britain by
Caledonian International Book Manufacturing Ltd, Glasgow

'Over the Bent World'
twenty-four poems by
Gerard Manley Hopkins

For Hans Rookmaaker

solway

'Over the Bent World'
twenty-four poems by
Gerard Manley Hopkins

Photographs by Tricia Porter

Commentary and Notes by David Porter

Contents

The Poems

Acknowledgements

We would like to thank the many people who have made this project possible and have given us advice, hospitality and the benefit of their knowledge of Hopkins. The following names are taken from a long list.

At Highgate School, the Principal Mr Kennedy, the Deputy Head Academic Katy Ricks and the school Archivist Mr Theodore Mallinson; at Balliol College Oxford, the Dean and Archivist Dr John Jones, the librarian Dr Penelope Bullock and her assistant Alan Tadiello; Joe and Linette Martin who provided 'wet weather' accommodation in Oxford; at Campion Hall Oxford, Fr Michael Suarez SJ; at the Birmingham Oratory the Rev C. J. G. Winterton who kindly sent us information and photographs; at Manresa House Roehampton, Mrs Alison Lawrence (Assistant/Secretary to the Estates Department of Roehampton campus, the University of Greenwich); at Stonyhurst College Fr Anthony Symondson SJ; at St Beuno's, Fr Damian Jackson SJ, Fr Michael O'Halloran SJ and Fr Michael Ivens SJ; in North Wales, John and Janet Robinson who provided us with accommodation (and information about Fynnon Fair and how to find it). Clergy, staff and helpers gave us help and information at a number of churches, including St Francis Xavier's Liverpool (where the staff provided us with by far the best cup of tea in the whole project) and St Aloysius' Church, Oxford. In Ireland we were given valuable help by the Curator of Newman House Dublin, Miss Ruth Ferguson; and at Monasterevan Mr Richard O'Rourke, Vice-President of the Gerard Manley Hopkins Society. Special thanks to Mrs Barbara Mainey of Dublin for hospitality and 'taxi' service.

We would also like to thank the many people who helped with, and sometimes modelled for, the photography, including Mrs Jill Mitchell who introduced us to local farrier Marcus Wehrle.

Not for the first time, we acknowledge with pleasure the help of the Petersfield Library, the Petersfield Bookshop, Bell's Bookshop and Alton Second-Hand Books; and thanks to Paul Clowney, Geoff Lovis and Gary Boxall for invaluable help on technical matters.

Among many friends and colleagues who have shared with us their love of, knowledge of and insights into Hopkins, not least are our publisher Pieter Kwant and his colleague Mark Finnie, both enthusiastic readers of Hopkins, and whose original idea this book was.

Finally, our younger daughter Lauren has been very long-suffering and a great help in preparing meals when work on the book overtook the household for quite a while; and our older daughter Ellie, returning home after her final year at University, put up with a house full of Hopkins with remarkable good humour.

Introduction

The poetry of Gerard Manley Hopkins is one of the curiosities with which literature abounds. During his lifetime and for years afterwards, the poetry of this learned, withdrawn Jesuit scholar was unknown to the public. Once in print, it rapidly became popular despite its rhythmic complexity, plentiful obscure references and avant-garde techniques. Today, in a Western world that has largely abandoned its Christian past, Hopkins's meditations on the ways of God and the intricate splendours of creation sell better than the work of many more conventional poets.

One reason is surely the sheer music of the poetry. Hopkins, who was keenly interested in music, had a good ear for melody in spoken words as well as in sung ones. Even readers unused to 'sprung rhythm' can readily respond to the lyrical celebration of 'The Windhover', the sadness of 'Binsey Poplars', the eloquent simplicity of the early poems such as 'Heaven-Haven' and the wonderful language of 'As kingfishers catch fire' (a poem that can be enjoyed for its evocative rich language quite apart from the fact that it is one of the key poems in which Hopkins expounds his philosophical doctrine of 'inscape').

This book is a celebration of Gerard Manley Hopkins. It's a book to dip into at random, to browse through or to read from beginning to end. We have resisted the temptation to write a brief life of Hopkins or a critical handbook to his work, though it has elements of both; we have chosen the poems to illustrate both Hopkins's life and his poetic development. We have not attempted to analyse his complex emotional and spiritual makeup, though we hope that the photographs and notes will help readers to understand a little more of these aspects of this often troubled poet. Readers who would like to explore any of these areas of Hopkins study will find the resources provided at the end of the book a useful starting point.

The photographs by Tricia Porter are a key part of the book. They are intended to be more than illustrations. Some of them depict places and people, and we have sometimes extended this by using contemporary illustrations. But most of the photographs are commentaries, explorations in visual terms of what Hopkins was communicating with words. We went to Stonyhurst College, for example, and photographed the distant hills from the same rooftop to which Hopkins often retreated. But for 'Inversnaid', we chose a local stream that shows very well the kind of features that struck Hopkins in the Scottish burn that today looks very different from how it did a century ago.

Captions to the photographs are supplied when they portray places mentioned in the text or where we felt that details of subject and location were of special interest. Most of the photographs, however, are intended to stand as images side by side with the text, without further commentary.

David and Tricia Porter

I have desired to go
Where springs not fail,
To fields where flies no sharp and sided hail
And a few lilies blow.

And I have asked to be
Where no storms come,
Where the green swell is in the havens dumb
And out of the swing of the sea.

Heaven-Haven (A nun takes the veil)

The Early Years

Childhood and Schooldays

Manley Hopkins was a successful London businessman whose marine insurance company was doing very well in 1844. But he can hardly have been surprised when his first child Gerard, born that year at the family home in Stratford, Essex, showed an early interest in poetry and art. It ran in the family; he himself had found time in a busy commercial life to publish several books, two of them collections of poetry, another the standard text on loss adjusting; and his wife Catherine had a great love of the arts.

Gerard's recent ancestors included the great Gainsborough and the Royal Academician Richard Lane; the roll-call of distinguished artistic Hopkinses included professional water-colourist Edward Smith and an aunt, Eleanor Hopkins, who was a gifted amateur. Gerard's mother encouraged his interest in poetry, though he was not the only one of her eight children to become successful in the arts. Arthur and Everard became painters and illustrators, Katie's skill at drawing was considerable, and Grace was musical. The youngest of the Hopkins children, Lionel, became a linguist. He was a world authority on the Chinese language, lived to a great age, survived World War II and died in 1952. Unusually for the family of a self-made businessman in the nineteenth century, only one of Manley's sons, Cyril, entered the family firm. Had Gerard's life developed differently, it would

Highgate Church during Hopkins's schooldays. At that time the school had no chapel; boys and masters worshipped here in the school pews. The school donated £2,000 for the building of the church.

12

have been an obvious choice of career for him as the oldest son.

Gerard's grandparents had been unable to send Manley, Gerard's father, to university. He had to build his business by hard work and flair. He was a typical Victorian self-made man, the kind of person of whom Samuel Smiles was to approve a few years later in such works as *Self-Help* and *Thrift*. He was also a God-fearing family man, whose churchmanship was in the Anglo-Catholic High Church and whose home was a pious one.

Gerard was like his parents in many ways. He displayed an independent streak like his father's, and was clearly gifted in a number of artistic disciplines. He was profoundly sensitive to beauty, often becoming emotionally distressed at particularly ugly scenes.

Dr John Bradley Dyne, Head Master 1838–74

His talent as a mimic and his musical interests both undoubtedly contributed to the technical achievements of his later poetry.

In 1852 the family moved to Hampstead and Gerard entered Sir Roger Cholmeley's School (now Highgate School) as a day boy. The school was an ancient institution (founded in 1565) but in Hopkins's time was recovering from years of decline; under its Headmaster John Dyne the numbers had risen from 19 pupils to well over 100. 'During his days,' wrote historian F. A. M. Webster, 'Highgate might justly be known as Dr Dyne's School.'

Dyne has left a mixed reputation behind him. A combination of the progressive and the old-fashioned, he was revered by some pupils as a beloved mentor out of the same mould as Tom Brown's Dr Arnold at Rugby School. But many of his charges disliked him. Between him and Gerard a particular mutual loathing seems to have built up. Gerard was an industrious pupil; his name appears very frequently as a borrower in the school library register, showing the determination and effort he gave his studies. But once, for a 'trifling' offence, Dyne punished him by forbidding him the use of a room that he was using to prepare for an important examination. It was a strange punishment to give a promising pupil, and Gerard was understandably aggrieved.

> Dyne and I had a terrific altercation. I was driven out of patience and cheeked him wildly, and he blazed into me with his riding-whip ... Shortly after ... like a fool I seized one of the upstairs candles on Sunday night when they had taken ours away too soon and my room was denied me ... Clarke, my co-victim, was flogged, struck off the confirmation list and fined £1;

13

> I was deprived of my room for ever, sent to bed at half-past nine
> till further orders, and ordered to work *only* in the school room,
> not even in the school library.

Gerard claimed that Dyne wanted him to do badly in his examinations. If that were so, the Headmaster's hopes were dashed when Gerard topped examination lists, and won academic prizes, a school scholarship and an Exhibition to Balliol College in Oxford. One prize was won with a poem, 'The Escorial'. He wrote other poems during his school career, one of which he illustrated, confirming a developing talent for drawing. The earliest poems, sometimes disconcertingly, give strong hints of the character of what was to follow. They are clearly the work of a schoolboy and are often technically uneven, but there are also passages that foreshadow the later Hopkins.

A Highgate School classroom today

At Highgate too he made long-standing friends. One was the poet, R. W. Dixon, who taught there in 1861 and was later to become an intimate correspondent and close friend. Ernest Hartley Coleridge, one of Gerard's closest friends at Highgate, was the grandson of the celebrated poet. Marcus Clarke went on to become a successful minor novelist.

Many of Gerard's contemporaries recall his fascination with painting, the drawings he brought back from family holidays at home and abroad (in 1857 he travelled abroad for the first time, touring Belgium and the Rhineland), and his ambition to become a professional painter.

R. W. Dixon gives a description of what Hopkins looked like as a schoolboy: 'A pale young boy, very light and active, with a very meditative and intellectual face.' (Many years later, Dixon told Hopkins that he still looked like the boy he had known at Highgate.) Nick-named 'Skin' Hopkins, Gerard was popular with his classmates. One of them, Charles Luxmoore, later de-scribed him as 'one of the very best and nicest boys in the school':

> Tenacious when duty was concerned, he was full of fun, rippling over with jokes, and chaff, facile with paper and pen, with rhyming jibe or cartoon; good, for his size, at games and taking his part, but not as we did placing them first. Quiet, gentle, always nice, and always doing his work well: I think he must have been a charming boy from a master's point of view, but he was completely changed by any wrong or ill treatment on their part.

Gerard Manley Hopkins aged 14½.
Portrait by his aunt, Eleanor Hopkins

He was a precocious, gifted young man. He had already made his mark in literature and was a high achiever academically. He had been brought up in an artistic and religious home in the High Anglican tradition, so had had ample opportunity to see the relationship between beauty and faith expressed in many ways. Oxford was a focus for many of the intellectual and artistic cross-currents of the age's ideas. It was the logical, perhaps necessary, next step.

One of a number of medals and other prizes that Gerard won at Highgate

The boughs, the boughs are bare enough
But earth has never felt the snow
Frost-furred our ivies are and rough ...

'Winter with the Gulf Stream'

First Publication

'Winter with the Gulf Stream' was published in the periodical *Once a Month* (to which Gerard's father was an occasional contributor) on St Valentine's Day 1863. The influence of Keats, strong in his early poems, is less strong in this one, though there is a clear influence of Tennyson. (Hopkins was good at writing pastiches of both.) But this poem has its own voice too.

The mature Hopkins is foreshadowed here in a number of ways. First, **the choice of form**. There is no hint of the metrical and rhythmic exploration that is to come later, but this writer knows poetic form and can use it to communicate meanings. He chooses the *terza rima* form, with its tight rhyme scheme and regular metre, but constantly challenges it. There is a pleasing ambiguity in the sequence 'boughs ... boughs ... enough ... snow ... rough ... shew', where rhymes appear to the eye that do not exist in the ear (for example 'bough/enough'). Then in the lines themselves Hopkins creates structures independent of the *terza rima* form, for example by using alliteration. 'Black branches', 'shot and shine', 'looks laid', and more all contribute to the poetic texture and to the metrical variety. Second, **the choice of words**. Already we see Hopkins's delight in sensuous language, couched in sharp observation. The reader's senses are involved: touch – 'frost-furred', hearing – 'the hoarse leaves crawl on hissing ground', and sight – 'the waxen colours weep and run'. Such acute descriptions occur throughout the poem. Third, **the use of invented words**. 'Slendering' (an extraordinarily effective word when you consider what it describes) is Hopkins's own creation. Fourth, **the use of compressed grammar**. 'In scarves of silky shot and shine' – of the many contemporary meanings of the word 'shot', which does Hopkins have in mind? A sudden stab of pain? A watery outflow? The silk fabric of that name? (And if the latter, is he using it as noun or adjective?) As is often the case with Hopkins's frequent later obscurities, you could re-write the line, perhaps as: 'The sun is dressed in beautiful silk scarves that shine.' But that would lose not only the poetic power, but the freedom for many meanings to co-exist. Does Hopkins mean the sun is dressed in silk and in (sun) shine, or is it the scarves that shine? You, the reader, do not have to choose. Both ideas work in your imagination to create the complex visual spectacle Hopkins wants you to 'see'.

Fifth, **the capacity of this poetry to move the reader**. There is no complexity or ambiguity in the beautiful couplet that ends the poem, stripped of punctuation and containing almost only single-syllable, simple words. Having resisted using his chosen verse form in a mechanical, predictable way, Hopkins now uses its traditional two-line conclusion brilliantly to describe the moment of simple darkness that follows the visual glory of the winter sunset.

Gerard was eighteen years old when this poem was published. It is one of a very small number published in his lifetime.

Winter with the Gulf Stream

The boughs, the boughs are bare enough
But earth has never felt the snow
Frost-furred our ivies are and rough

With bills of rime the brambles shew.
The hoarse leaves crawl on hissing ground
Because the sighing wind is low.

But if the rain-blasts be unbound
And from dank feathers wring the drops
The clogged brook runs with choking sound

Kneading the mounded mire that stops
His channel under clammy coats
Of foliage fallen in the copse.

A simple passage of weak notes
Is all the winter bird dare try,
The bugle moon by daylight floats

So glassy white about the sky,
So like a berg of hyaline,
And pencilled blue so daintily,

I never saw her so divine.
But through black branches, rarely drest
In scarves of silky shot and shine,

The webbed and the watery west
Where yonder crimson fireball sets
Looks laid for feasting and for rest.

I see long reefs of Violets
In beryl-covered fens so dim,
A gold-water Pactolus frets

Its brindled wharves and yellow brim,
The waxen colours weep and run,
And slendering to his burning rim

Into the flat blue mist the sun
Drops out and all our day is done.

Pactolus King Midas, offered his wish, asked that everything he touched might turn to gold. When that turned out to be an unbearable liability he was told to bathe in the River Pactolus to rid himself of it. Hence the Pactolus's proverbial golden sands.

Balliol College, Oxford

Oxford Foundations

Benjamin Jowett (1817-93), from a photograph by H. Hay Cameron. Jowett was Professor of Greek when Hopkins was an undergraduate

When Gerard Manley Hopkins left Sir Roger Cholmeley's School in Highgate, his experiences there had prepared him exceptionally well for the literary life. He had been blessed with extensive family connections with the arts; a creatively entrepreneurial father and an artistic, supportive mother; friends at school who were also inclined to literature; and the kind of education that had sharpened his eyes, ears and intellect to the kind of perception that poetry demands. He had read widely and perceptively, and the results showed in his writing. Add to that the prizes he had already gained for poetry, his publication in *Once a Month* and the admiration that his poems had already won, and he looked set for a celebrated career as a writer.

A clue to what actually lay ahead might be that at Highgate he had been admired by some of his classmates for his determination to keep a solemn promise made to his mother, that he would read a part of the Bible each night before sleeping. He handled the teasing that this provoked so well that the others in his dormitory decided that honour was satisfied; the intention of keeping a promise was adequate excuse for such strange behaviour.

He had also shown the tenacity that the artistic life requires. There is a well-known story that he bet a friend half a sovereign that he could go without any liquids at all for an extended period. He stuck to his vow until his tongue turned black, then collapsed during school drill. Dyne punished him ruthlessly; people said that it was that incident which started their mutual dislike. The Head might have done better to have given some thought to the unusual character of a boy who could make such a vow and keep it.

If the intellectual and moral foundations of the later Jesuit priest and poet had begun to be laid, the beginnings of a complex, perceptive personality had also begun to form. Sensitive often to the point of tears, he was also regarded by his school friends as full of fun and having a wicked sense of humour. In later life, too, he occasionally displayed a dry waggishness, but – as portraits of the young Gerard confirm – from childhood there was always a certain amount of insecurity behind his clear, rather distant eyes.

Legends

Oxford in 1863 was populated by scholarly legends. Matthew Arnold was Professor of Poetry. The Professor of Hebrew was the internationally famous scholar and preacher Edward Pusey, and the Professor of Greek was the equally celebrated Benjamin Jowett, translator of Plato, and destined to become Master of Balliol – to which college he had been elected a Fellow while still an undergraduate. The controversial John Keble was back in Oxford. John Newman, since 1845 the most famous English convert to Roman Catholicism of all time, was now in Birmingham at the Oratory he had founded, but had left behind him in Oxford the influence of a brilliant academic career, his dramatic conversion, and a growing reputation from his writings on education.

These and others like them were key players in some of the great church controversies of the nineteenth century. But they were also great scholars, and it was as such that they made their first impact on Hopkins. At Highgate, he had struggled under the discipline of a headmaster he despised. At Balliol he had the opportunity to listen to teachers he revered.

He blossomed. His rooms became the setting for social gatherings of all kinds, and he was a popular guest at other students' parties. But he also plunged into study, reading voraciously and grasping every intellectual opportunity that Oxford offered. He also began to keep a journal and to make detailed notes, documenting

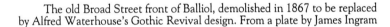

The old Broad Street front of Balliol, demolished in 1867 to be replaced by Alfred Waterhouse's Gothic Revival design. From a plate by James Ingram

John Newman

Edward Pusey

the meanings of words and also noting his own perceptions and descriptions. Here is a fragment of his meticulous analysis of the derivation of the English word 'horn':

> From its being the highest point comes our *crown* perhaps, in the sense of the top of the head, and the Greek κέραξ, horn, and κάρα, head, were evidently identical; then for its sprouting up and growing, compare *keren, cornu,* κέραξ, horn with grow, *cresco, grandis,* grass, great, *groot.* For its curving, *curvus* is probably from the root *horn* in one of its forms. κορωνη in Greek and *corvus, cornix* in Latin and *crow* (perhaps also *raven,* which may have been *craven* originally) in English bear a striking resemblance to *cornu, curvus* ...

He also made careful notes of his observations of nature and the created world, many of which in due course became poems. In spring 1864 he jotted down the comment: 'Moonlight hanging or dropping on treetops like blue cobwebs', and, watching rowers on the river, noted that 'the beaded oar, dripping, powders or sows the smooth with watery drops'.

And he wrote letters. Hopkins's letters to his small circle of friends are the most important resource for understanding his work and his life. We do not have the legacy of intimate family letters that we possess in the case of some major poets, but his letters to friends are full of detail, discussion and debate.

The Test Acts

The Test Acts of 1673 and 1678 were an attempt to prevent 'Romish con-spiracies'. The first Test Act excluded from public office anybody who refused to swear allegiance to the crown, acknowledge crown supremacy, declare that they disbelieved in transubstantiation, and receive communion in the Church of England. This substantial disadvantage to England's Roman Catholics was followed by the second Test Act of 1678, which required all members of the House of Commons and the Lords to make anti-Catholic and royalist declara-tions before they could take their seats.

In the 1720s a series of Indemnity Acts made some attempts to reduce the draconian measures of the first Test Act; but it was not until a century later, in 1828, that the Test and Corporation Acts repealed the 1673 Act and allowed Roman Catholics to hold office. The Catholic Emancipation Act of 1829 – passed in an atmosphere of public concern over potentially inflammable events in Ireland – allowed Roman Catholics to sit in Parliament and to hold most of the high offices of state.

It was not until 1871, however, some years after Gerard Manley Hopkins graduated, that the University Test Acts finally made it possible for Roman Catholics (and Nonconformists) to teach at Oxford and Cambridge.

This document, issued in 1688 to the author's ancestor, Sir John Tyas of Worcester, confirmed that having taken communion in his parish church 'according to the usage of the Church of England', he was now eligible to hold civil or military office

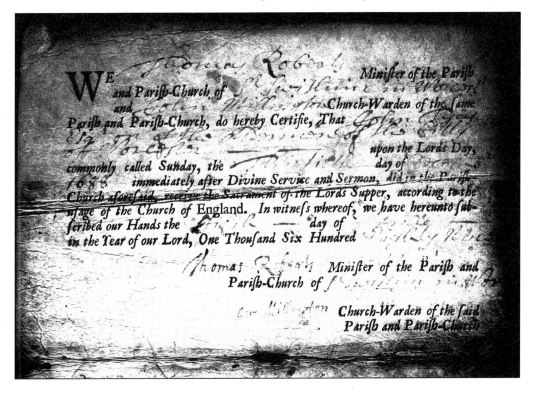

Cross-Currents

Oxford in 1863 was changing, but much of it remained as it had for centuries. In 'Duns Scotus's Oxford' (p. 99) Hopkins portrays a 'towery city' whose ancient spires, green spaces and mediaeval alleyways still looked much as Scotus knew them. The explosion of architecture that would transform Oxford still lay a few years in the future, and there was much to delight Hopkins's eye as he walked and sketched in the city and its surroundings.

There were less visible changes imminent than architectural ones, however. The Master of Balliol, like his predecessors, was a clergyman: at Oxford, as in Victorian England generally, religion was the core of life, and kept there by the University Test Acts which still ensured that every don was a member of the Church of England.

In that Church several movements were growing. The Evangelical movement taught that the centre of the Christian faith was neither the sacraments nor ritual, but the reading and practice of the Bible. Evangelicals also taught the value of preaching and home Bible study, and emphasised evangelism as a Christian obligation and duty. The Evangelical Alliance, founded in 1846, was a movement against Catholicism, drawing its membership from all sectors of the Protestant church (today the Alliance speaks on social, ethical and other issues for a broad, and large, constituency of British Evangelicals). The Church Missionary Society

A sketch of the new 1876 Oxford by Kate Hopkins, from a scrapbook in Balliol library

had been formed in 1798 and had already achieved great success in preaching the gospel in foreign lands.

The Church of England, with its historic claim to 'comprehensiveness' (a commitment to what may be considered the essentials of the faith, while remaining flexible about other matters) accommodated a wide variety of protestant Christian belief; even the rise of Nonconformist influence, through movements like the growing Evangelical Alliance, would probably not have greatly weakened it.

But another force for change was growing; and it was growing in Oxford.

As long ago as the 1830s a High Anglican movement had been prominent in Oxford church life and was exerting a much wider influence as well. It had begun at Oriel College, with a circle of young Anglicans whose leader was John Keble. Keble's 1833 'Assize Sermon', on national apostasy, had galvanised them into a movement for the return to biblical purity in the church, based on a view of authority based on apostolic succession. One of them, John Henry Newman, launched a series of 'Tracts for the Times', and the Oxford Movement was born. Its key names are John Newman, John Keble, Edward Pusey and Richard Froude.

It is ironic that a movement with such a high view of the authority of bishops should have met with increasing resistance by the bishops of the Church of England, culminating when Newman produced his *Tract 90* in 1841. He argued that the Anglican Thirty-Nine Articles were (apart from a few 'minor errors' that had crept in over the years) compatible with Roman Catholic teaching. He thereby lost the last vestige of Evangelical support and set the Movement into direct confrontation with the bishops.

Its critics dubbed the 'Tractarians' covert Roman Catholics, and many Evangelicals reacted by aligning themselves with the Nonconformists. A dangerous split developed in Anglicanism, highlighted in 1845 when Newman converted to Rome, taking many of his supporters with him. Keble and Pusey stayed within the established Church as campaigners for the High Church movement.

The Oxford Movement had some significant consequences: the further growth of Nonconformity, the rise of Christian Socialism, and the rise of a distinctive philosophy of education in the work of writers like Charles Kingsley, F. W. Farrar and Talbot Baines Reed. The Church of England emerged dominated by the Liberal, Broad Church movement.

Above: a Balliol gargoyle

Taking Sides

Hopkins's upbringing predisposed him to the High Church movement, an inclination encouraged by his discovery of the Pre-Raphaelite movement in art and literature. He was fascinated by the Oxford Movement. Benjamin Jowett, Professor of Greek at Balliol, was an antagonist of Pusey, who since Newman's conversion represented the most brilliant and articulate champion of the High Church cause. Jowett advocated a broad church, welcoming all shades of believer. Hopkins – influenced again perhaps by the fact that his tutor James Riddell, a charismatic and attractive personality, was a 'Puseyite' – gravitated in the direction of Pusey and his followers.

A major attraction was the even more magnetic character of Henry Liddon, who preached regularly to large student congregations at St Mary's where Newman had been vicar at the time of his conversion. Preachers like Liddon were much needed, for the Oxford Movement had somewhat lost steam, and ritual had

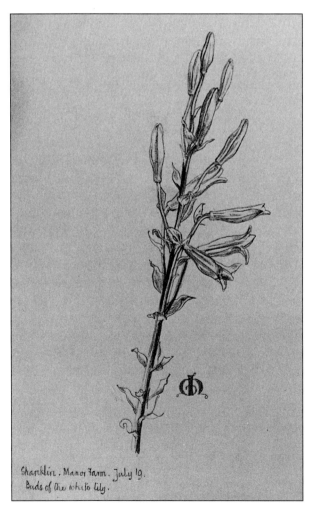

Shanklin. Manor Farm. July 19.
Buds of the white lily.

A sketch made by Hopkins during a family holiday on the Isle of Wight in his first Oxford Long Vacation

28

replaced piety and fervour for many of its members. Overemphasis on the externals, on incense, vestments, and other peripherals had gained some of its members the nickname 'Ritualists'. They had moved away from the original desire to purify the Church and return to catholic roots and the ideals of primitive Christianity, to stand against national spiritual decline as Keble had urged they should. Pusey and his associates recognised the danger and preached against it. The Movement's critics, such as Jowett, were trenchant in their criticism.

Among Hopkins's close friends were several 'Liddonites', such as the poet and athlete Robert Bridges (an attraction of opposites, for he was unlike Hopkins in many ways), William Addis, a theologian whom he admired greatly, and William Urquart, who was at that time torn between allegiance to Anglicanism and Roman Catholicism. No such inner turmoil afflicted Mowbray Baillie, a fellow undergraduate at Balliol, who believed religion to be irrational. Friendship grew over much amicable wrangling and some determined efforts by Hopkins to convince his friend that religion transcends, rather than replaces, common sense.

During the years of searching Hopkins continued to sketch, foreshadowing the 'inscape' and 'instress' of the later poems

He had other, non-Liddonite friends, such as the Evangelical Martin Geldart, also of Balliol. It was an unlikely friendship. Geldart hated his time at Oxford, being obsessed with an awareness of his own sinfulness. Years later he wrote his autobiography, *A Son of Belial*, under the pseudonym of Nitram Tradleg. Hopkins appears as 'Gerontius Manley ... my ritualistic friend'.

By 1864 Hopkins was calling himself a Tractarian, though he had as yet no clear idea where his future church allegiance should be. He began to practise some ascetic exercises, such as fasting and 'depriving himself of beauty' for periods of time. When not depriving himself he wrote and sketched enthusiastically and copiously. A family holiday in the Isle of Wight at the end of his first year inspired him, but the real inspiration was the fertile intellectual and spiritual landscape of Oxford.

His academic work was prospering too: Jowett dubbed him 'the star of Balliol', and arranged for him to be taught by Walter Pater of Brasenose College, who was for many undergraduates the high priest of beauty. 'To burn always with this hard gem-like flame,' Pater wrote in *Studies in the History of the Renaissance*, 'to maintain this ecstasy, is success in life.' On its publication in 1873, after Hopkins had graduated, this collection of essays became instantly one of the most widely read and influential books in Oxford.

So there were influences on Hopkins from a number of directions. His notebooks show his increasing awareness of beauty as he studied, read and simply walked and looked. His daily habits were changing under the influence of the Puseyites and Liddon; he began to go to confession, and his mother was horrified to discover that he was fasting regularly and abstaining from meat on Fridays. But it would be wrong to assume that he was so devoted to the Oxford Movement that Jowett and Pater were lesser influences. He admired Jowett and acknowledged his 'purity', and some of Jowett's more biting criticisms of the Tractarians and their followers must have hit uncomfortably close to home. But his direction was becoming clearer with every week that passed.

Alleyways like these, despite the modern encumbrances, are a reminder of how past and present have always co-existed in Oxford

Portrait of John Henry Newman
in Newman House, Dublin

'Very Reverend Father,

I have been up at Oxford just long enough to have heard fr. my father and mother in return for my letter announcing my conversion. Their answers are terrible; I cannot read them twice. If you will pray for them and me just now I shall be deeply thankful ...'

Letter to John Henry Newman, 15 October 1866

Conversion, and the Jesuits

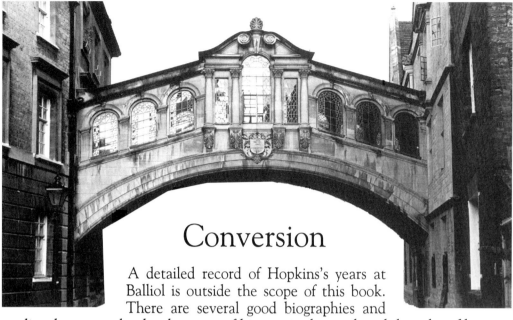

Conversion

A detailed record of Hopkins's years at Balliol is outside the scope of this book. There are several good biographies and studies that trace the development of his poetic theory, his philosophy of beauty, his various friendships and many other aspects of this crucial time in his life. The story of his gradual journey towards the Roman Catholic Church has also often been told.

The best account of his development, however, is to be found in his letters, notebooks and the journals that he kept during his Oxford years. In them we see him exploring new worlds of knowledge, going to musical performances and writing down his comments, meeting famous writers like the Rossettis, and constantly examining and scrutinising images and words. He fills pages with carefully observed sketches, and in two tiny notebooks poems are written in odd spaces between other notes. It is in these writings that we see his notes to himself as reminders of the various abstinences, the beginnings of pessimism, and methodical notes on the weather.

He was beginning to realise that he would probably never be a professional artist like his brothers, though he still wrote about his own and others' art. What he was going to be was far from clear, though he was an outstanding student and had a wide choice of stimulating and profitable careers waiting for him. His position in the religious controversies of Oxford was taking shape; he admired the 'purity' of Jowett, but was drawn to Pusey, who was regarded as defending the historic Anglican Middle Way, the *via media*, against the pull of Rome, Broad Churchmanship, Evangelicalism, and more.

The reasons that made him choose to enter the Church of Rome are complex. But there is no doubt that one person exerted an overwhelming influence: John Henry Newman. The single event that probably counted most in Hopkins's decision was the publication in 1864, in response to a challenge by writer Charles Kingsley, of Newman's *Apologia Pro Vita Sua*. This account of his conversion to Roman

Catholicism became a national best-seller and strengthened immeasurably the Catholic cause in Britain.

Newman's winsome personality was itself an answer to some of Kingsley's more savage charges. He argued that the Middle Way of High Anglicanism could no longer be defended as the repository of historic, New Testament Christianity. The few doubts he had expressed in *Tract 90* he had now settled in his own mind. If Rome and Canterbury were mutually compatible, then, argued Newman, one should choose Rome, as manifestly the more historic of the two. That was why he had made the ultimate decision, to enter the Church of Rome.

It was a crucial step in Hopkins's own conversion, for it appealed to the test of authority, which for him, Newman and many other famous converts such as G. K. Chesterton, was the supreme advantage of Rome. He thought a great deal, agonised much, talked and wrote to friends and counsellors and finally in August 1866 approached Newman himself. His mind was made up, he said; Newman would not have to convince him of anything. He wanted to be received into the Church of Rome.

His parents were devastated. 'Gerard, my darling boy, are you indeed gone from me?', wrote his father. (Catherine Phillips, in her World's Classics edition of the *Poems*, suggests that Hopkins's mother may have drafted the letter.) Friends attempted to dissuade him when they knew of his intention. Liddon, unavoidably absent from Oxford at the time, wrote three letters in four days, desperately trying to persuade him to change his mind. Pusey, whose Anglo-Catholicism never led him to abandon the Church of England, was bitterly hurt and rejected Hopkins's attempt to explain himself.

Hopkins knew that he was turning his back on a future, too; a minority church, disadvantaged and under-resourced, was his future now, not the prosperous pastures of Anglicanism. But, he wrote to his father,

> I am most anxious that you shd. not think of my future. It is likely that the positions you wd. like to see me in wd. have no attraction for me, and surely the happiness of my prospects depends on the happiness to me and not on intrinsic advantages. It is possible even to be very sad and very happy at once.

• • •

Extraordinarily, for one who had undergone such spiritual and mental turmoil, Hopkins fulfilled expectations less than a year later by graduating with a first-class degree. He accepted an invitation from Newman to teach for several months in Birmingham at the Oratory school. By May 1868 he had made up his mind to become a priest.

Above left; the 'Bridge of Sighs', Oxford

To the Priesthood

Hopkins had clearly been interested in the idea of entering the priesthood since at least the time of his conversion. In a poem of the same year, 'The Habit of Perfection', he uses images of the priesthood; and in 'Heaven-Haven' (included in this book on p. 10 as the first of our chosen poems) he obviously feels that the contemplative life offers longed-for spiritual rewards and peace.

'The Habit of Perfection' is printed overleaf. Reading it is a sombre and uplifting experience; sombre, because it is a poem about loss (loss of sensual gratification, not necessarily in a bad way), and uplifting, because Hopkins proposes a greater benefit for each of the things lost. In place of the joys of the cultivated palate (Hopkins's wine parties had been legendary at Balliol) is the sharpened taste of the spiritual food that rewards those who fast. The hands and feet that had delighted in strolling the meadows and lawns of Oxford would now experience the joys of walking the 'golden street' before the altar of God. In place of rich robes, the supplicant will be dressed in lily-white robes of poverty. And so on, for each of the five senses.

One by one, Hopkins offers up those senses in sacrifice, and takes his reward. For example, at the time of writing the poem he was deeply fond of music; but the 'Elected Silence' is to be the music that is the real music, 'the music that I care to hear'. In fact, having made the sacrifice himself, music was given back to him; in 1868 he wrote to Baillie from Birmingham and mentioned that he had begun to learn the violin ('I am glad I have') though the intention was unable to survive the teaching workload. His love of music, in many forms, continued for the rest of his life. He might well have echoed the words of Jesus, which must have been in his mind constantly in these years:

> Verily I say unto you, There is no man that hath left house, or brethren, or sisters, or father, or mother, or wife, or children, or lands, for my sake, and the gospel's, but he shall receive an hundredfold now in this time, houses, and brethren, and sisters, and mothers, and children, and lands, with persecutions; and in the world to come eternal life (Mark 10:29,30).

The poem, of course, is an abstract meditation on the call to the priesthood, and is neither a manifesto nor a confession. But it is a moving insight into the mind of the convert, already grappling with the known and unknown consequences of becoming a Catholic, as he contemplates the cost of the further commitment to the priesthood.

The Society of Jesus

The future was now a major issue. Hopkins frankly did not much enjoy his teaching at the Oratory, and missed the intellectual and artistic stimulus of Oxford. He was not banned from the family home (provided, said his father, that he did not attempt to convert his brothers), and had spent his first Christmas as a Catholic at home in Hampstead. But he was by now sure that he should not pursue his ambition of following his gifted brothers and becoming a painter, which had survived his schooldays and most of his time as an undergraduate. 'The higher and more attractive parts of the art put a strain upon the passions which I shd. think it unsafe to encounter.'

His university friends were launching their careers. Hopkins could have done likewise. Though an Oxford or Cambridge teaching post was not open to him, life was easier for English Catholics now than it had been at the time of Newman's conversion, and the priesthood was not the only option. It was, like most of Hopkins's career moves, a deliberate and deeply thought-out choice.

He was drawn to the priesthood for several reasons; and there were several reasons to make him think twice before making such a momentous step. He would probably, he knew, be allowed to continue his writing. Becoming a priest would enable him to dedicate his life entirely to God. There would be structure and discipline too, which Hopkins craved just as he had embraced the authority of the Church of Rome and rejected what he regarded as the unsubstantiated claims to authority of the Church of England. His longing for beauty, his enjoyment of the classics, his passion for nature and the voice of God in creation – all these could be satisfied, and deeply satisfied, as a priest.

On the other hand, he knew it would break his mother's heart.

And what sort of priest should he become? He considered the comfortable life at the Oratory that would be open to him once he had shed the onerous teaching work and become a fully-fledged priest. The Benedictines were an option too, with their long history in Oxford and relatively open structure. And the Society of Jesus, the Jesuits, offered years of study, rigorous discipline, and life-long vows of chastity, celibacy and obedience. If Hopkins wanted structure and discipline, he would find them in abundance in the Jesuits.

'I think it is the very thing for you,' wrote Newman when in May 1868 he heard that Hopkins had chosen to join the Jesuits. 'Don't call the Jesuit discipline hard, it will bring you to heaven. The Benedictines would not have suited you.'

He treasured Newman's approval, but was even more touched by his parents' understanding, and the 'kind and contented way' in which they had taken the news.

Almost his last act before entering the Jesuit novitiate was to burn his poems. Only drafts in notebooks, copies sent to friends and some alternative versions escaped the flames. It was not part of the Jesuit discipline. He did it because 'they wd. interfere with my state and vocation.' The poem overleaf is one of just four 'early poems' that Robert Bridges felt able to include in the first 'complete' edition of Gerard Manley Hopkins's poems, published in 1918.

The Habit of Perfection

Elected Silence, sing to me
And beat upon my whorlèd ear,
Pipe me to pastures still and be
The music that I care to hear.

Shape nothing, lips; be lovely-dumb:
It is the shut, the curfew sent
From there where all surrenders come
Which only makes you eloquent.

Be shellèd, eyes, with double dark
And find the uncreated light:
This ruck and reel which you remark
Coils, keeps, and teases simple sight.

Palate, the hutch of tasty lust,
Desire not to be rinsed with wine:
The can must be so sweet, the crust
So fresh that come in fasts divine!

Nostrils, your careless breath that spend
Upon the stir and keep of pride,
What relish shall the censers send
Along the sanctuary side!

O feel-of-primrose hands, O feet
That want the yield of plushy sward,
But you shall walk the golden street
And you unhouse and house the Lord.

And, Poverty, be thou the bride
And now the marriage feast begun,
And lily-coloured clothes provide
Your spouse not laboured-at nor spun.

Whorled Coiled or spiralled, esp. in ridges.
Ruck and reel Typically, this combines several
associations, for example 'ruck' = rugby
scrum, 'reel' = a strenuous dance; the bustle of
everyday life hinders 'simple sight'.
Censers A neat comparison, for the smell of
incense in a censer is acrid and pungent;
hence a keener experience for the senses.
Unhouse and house the Lord A reference to
the administration of the sacraments from the
altar, and a possible indication that priesthood
was in Hopkins's mind in January 1866.

Left: church porch, Selborne, Hampshire

The Novitiate

The procedures and formalities of acceptance as a Jesuit novice went smoothly. Hopkins spent a summer holiday in Switzerland with his friend Edward Bond who was – perhaps significantly – by no means the most religious of his friends. The choice of holiday was certainly significant. Jesuits were forbidden entry to Switzerland. Hopkins was seeing the Alps for the last time.

On his return he set his affairs in order and made his farewells, almost as if leaving this world, which in a sense he was. The life of a Jesuit novice is an enclosed one: two years of menial work and spiritual exercise, in which the overall purpose is to teach unquestioning obedience and a complete understanding of what the Jesuit life entails and demands.

Manresa House, where Hopkins spent the next two years, is an eighteenth-century mansion in Roehampton in south London. Built originally for the Earls of Bessborough, it was sold in 1861 to the Jesuits. The circumstances of the sale are still not fully known. As Jesuits were discriminated against in many ways (they were specifically excluded from the Catholic Emancipation Act) the negotiations had to take place in secrecy, through intermediaries. So unpopular was the Society that it was said that Queen Victoria planted a row of trees in Richmond Park to hide Manresa House from her view.

Once installed, the new owners embarked on extensive alterations and expansions, turning the building into a secluded, enclosed house. They called it Manresa House after the place in Spain where Ignatius Loyola wrote his *Spiritual Exercises*, the foundational text of the Society of Jesus and the basis of thirty days of intense spiritual meditation and soul-searching that was the first stage of the novitiate.

The month spent studying the *Exercises* was the prelude to two hard years in which the novices' day stretched from 5.30 am to 10 pm, during which time they laboured at gardening, manual work, kitchen work, cleaning and all the other tasks a large house and community require. The only conversation allowed was for forty-five minutes after supper; the meal itself, like all the meals, was eaten in silence, unless a spiritual book was being read aloud to the novices.

The physical discomfort was matched by the intellectual and cultural deprivation. This was not a time for academic study. The brilliant student who had graduated the previous year with a double first spent more time cleaning lavatories than reading the classics. ('The slate slabs of the urinals ... are frosted in graceful sprays,' Hopkins noted in his journal.) Newspapers were forbidden, as was all secular reading. Walks on the common were occasionally allowed, but only in groups of three and those three had to be chosen by the Master of Novices. Once a year the novices were given a small amount of pocket money and allowed out to visit art galleries, museums and the aquarium.

'During the entire time I was here we never did one creative thing,' one novice recalls. 'We were even forbidden to look out of the window.' Certainly Hopkins

Opposite: staircase in Manresa House, Roehampton

wrote no poems during the two years, though he did make some useful observations that later appear in poems: the 'roundy wells' of 'As kingfishers catch fire' (p. 89) are based on the Manresa well, said to be the deepest in London. Novices were allowed to throw stones down it and were given dire warnings that if they failed the novitiate, they would also be thrown into the well. It says much for the rigours of the novitiate that some of them believed it.

St Mary's Hall, Stonyhurst

The obituary of Gerard Manley Hopkins in the Jesuit periodical *Letters and Notices* (September 1889) observes: 'His fellow-novices well remember his panegyric of St Stanislaus, which was as brilliant and beautiful as it was out of the usual routine of pulpit deliveries.' The two years at Roehampton had been ones in which such intellectual and creative qualities had been necessarily suppressed. At the end of his novitiate, having taken the vows of poverty, chastity and perpetual obedience, he could now look forward to returning to academic study as he entered the next stage of his training.

University graduates who had taken their first vows were judged sufficiently academically equipped not to need the 'juniorate' stage of further education; they proceeded immediately to a course in philosophy. 'Sept 9, 1870 – To Stonyhurst to the Seminary,' Gerard noted in his journal, and arrived at St Mary's Hall, Stonyhurst, Lancashire, ready to embark on three years of study.

His spirits and imagination lifted, not only after the hard regime at Manresa House, but also because he was in the northern countryside after two years in a London suburb. He loved Pendle Hill, a constant backdrop to his daily activities and plainly visible from the window of his room. At Roehampton walking in the rural city outskirts had been a rare treat; now he had leisure times when he could roam in nearby Clitheroe, Whalley, Whitewell and many more places. His journals and notebooks at this period are much fuller than those of the previous two years. He also became fascinated with the local Lancashire dialect, which, characteristically, he set about recording. Dialect became almost a hobby for him; his letters often mention interesting accents, and he was working on a substantial project on the subject when he died.

There were many pleasures at St Mary's that he had not enjoyed for a while. He was able to travel, and his family was able to visit him. He got to some art exhibitions. His teachers were unusually enlightened; aware that the course was a demanding one, they encouraged students to use their recreation time profitably. There were fishing expeditions, trips to places like the Isle of Man, and a good deal of sketching. Music, too, was allowed, and the rigorously controlled socialising of Roehampton was replaced by a congenial atmosphere in which friendships flourished.

On the other hand, it was a period of very poor health for Hopkins, whose constitution was weakened by the northern climate aggravating a chronic haemorrhoid condition. A chill developed into something more serious, and an operation became necessary. Convalescing at the family home in Hampstead he

was visited by several of his old Oxford friends, including Mowbray Baillie and Edward Bond.

The three years at St Mary's were years without poetry. But Hopkins was filling pages of his journal and notebooks with meticulous notes and observations. It was a treasure-trove of which he was later to make good use. But there was also developing that other trait that would characterise his mature poetry – a streak of sadness, even depression. To an extent it was part of his very emotional personality: at Manresa House and also at Stonyhurst he had been sometimes moved to tears by moments of spiritual clarity and perception. It was also the product of his frequent illnesses, which tended to leave him physically weak and spiritually depressed. This had an impact on his perceptions:

> Being unwell I was quite downcast: nature in all her parcels and
> faculties gaped and fell apart, *fatiscebat*, like a clod cleaving and
> holding only by strings of root. But this must often be.

He was depressed, too, by the knowledge that so many people either refused to acknowledge, or lacked awareness of, God's speaking presence all around them, in the simplest things:

> I thought how sadly beauty of inscape was unknown and buried
> away from simple people, and yet how near at hand it was if they
> had eyes to see it and it could be called out everywhere again.

Inscape and Instress

In 1872 Hopkins, as part of his philosophy studies at Stonyhurst, came across the work of a thirteenth-century Franciscan. As he turned the pages of Duns Scotus's commentary on the Sentences of Peter Lombard he realised, with all the thrill of a great discovery, that he was reading the words of somebody who saw the world in the same terms as he did. He now knew that he was not alone in seeking out the 'inscape' of things. At least one other, and that person a great father of the mediaeval church, had also sensed the presence of God defining and shaping the very creation itself.

Not much is known of the life of John Duns Scotus (c.1265-1308). He was probably born in Duns in Berwickshire, he was ordained priest in Northampton, and he taught in Oxford, probably in Cambridge, and certainly in Paris and Cologne, where he died. Many of his writings were unfinished. His major works have come down to us as transcripts of his lectures, usually transcribed by his students. But Duns Scotus is remembered as 'the subtle doctor', one of the two greatest theologians of the Middle Ages, though the English Reformers despised him and the contemptuous name they gave his followers – 'dunces' – is now part of the English language. Hopkins, however, revered him, and considered him 'of realty the rarest-veined traveller'.

For Duns Scotus, the natural world was the consequence of God's will – the primary creative force in nature. And to understand nature you have to look, Scotus argued, not at what something's name is, or the category to which it belongs, but what it does. To this understanding Hopkins brought a sharp eye and an acute awareness of the true appearance of things. In Hopkins, the 'inscape' of a thing is that which defines it, and goes on defining it; there is an energy in it that keeps it what it is and stops it becoming some other thing. So in the meticulous, brilliantly observed perceptions of nature and the created world in his poetry, Hopkins is not just painting beautiful pictures in words, but is reaching towards the very essence of what he is describing. All the varied details and aspects of the thing described are not decorative embellishments but a harmonious system, the product of which is a uniqueness that separates the thing observed from everything else. (The word Scotus used for this is best translated 'this-ness'.)

Related to 'inscape' is 'instress', by which Hopkins meant a movement from deep within the object being looked at, into the depths of the observer's being. If inscape was a matter of observing and identifying the essence of something, then instress was a matter of feeling. It meant making contact with the energy that held the inscape in balance, a contact often reinforced by a spiritual perception that enabled the mind of the observer to embrace and experience the inscape directly. So if inscape is what holds something together and establishes its unique identity and essence, instress is what establishes the spiritual contact between what is seen and the one who sees. And this is true whether the object in question is a dragonfly, a kingfisher, or the grandeur of God.

'I do not think I have ever seen anything more beautiful than the bluebell I have been looking at. I know the beauty of the Lord by it ...'

Journal, 18 May 1870

The nature poetry of Gerard Manley Hopkins, for all its attention to detail and meticulous survey of appearances, does not belong with the writers of the eighteenth and nineteenth centuries who are sometimes called 'the poets of the microscope'. They used the new empirical science to record, often for the first time, the facts and the operations of nature. Gilbert White in Selborne meticulously noted down the migration patterns of swallows in his diary. James Thomson described winter storms. The Evangelical James Hervey and his spiritual and poetic heir William Cowper both brought a sharp eye to nature, often describing it in terms that have as much to do with scientific analysis as poetic flight. But Hopkins is intent on looking past the appearances, into the heart of things, and his motive for doing so is entirely religious. He wants to see the hand of God.

The diaries and notebooks that Hopkins kept, and the letters that he wrote, had often used the vocabulary of inscape and instress (and another Hopkins coinage, 'pitch', expressing a defining assertiveness: positive action of all kinds, described by Hopkins as 'the doing-be'). Scotus gave him a theological location and endorsement for things he had long felt. He was drawn much more to this Franciscan model than to the other great theologian, Thomas Aquinas, who was more to the Jesuit taste. Aquinas's model of a realm of nature and a realm of grace, with little interplay, was not so much to Hopkins's liking as was Scotus's vision of God energetically present at every hand.

Although Hopkins never explains his poetical philosophy in terms that make it easy to grasp, it becomes much less fearsome when one realises that it was not a wholly new concept. Hopkins's work has many links with much more familiar poetry. When Wordsworth, for example, wrote 'One impulse from a vernal wood/May teach you more of man,/Of moral evil and of good,/Than all the sages can,' he was, strictly speaking, talking about the capacity of nature to instruct morally, but the concept is very close to Hopkins's inscape. And the moment of instress is very close to Wordsworth's 'spots of time', which he describes in Book XII of 'The Prelude' as possessing a 'renovating virtue'; or to James Joyce's 'epiphanies'. Joyce defined 'epiphany' in very Hopkinsesque style. He called it the 'sudden revelation of the whatness of a thing', when 'the soul of the commonest object seems to us radiant'.

It is the parallels between Hopkins's solitary pursuit of beauty and inscape, and the work of poets like Wordsworth, Yeats and many more, that establishes him as a significant figure in the Romantic movement. He regarded inscape as the essential quality of poetry, dismissing verse that lacked it as 'Parnassian'. 'Poetry is in fact speech employed to carry the inscape of speech for the inscape's sake.' The result, for Hopkins, was an aestheticism that had some similarities to the Romantic view of inspiration.

What made his poetic views distinctive, however, was his conviction that inscape and instress were both inseparable from the works of God. If you understood the inscape of a thing, if you had experienced instress, you had grown spiritually; you knew a little more about the ways of God in creation. The converse was also true: failure to perceive these things was spiritually dangerous. In a similar way, the poet William Cowper – who, like Gerard Manley Hopkins, endured periodic bouts of depression – had written eighty years earlier:

In one day, in one moment I should rather have said, [Nature] became an universal blank to me ... Why is scenery like this, I had almost said, why is this very scene, which many years since I could not contemplate without rapture, now become, at the best, an insipid wilderness to me? ... The reason is obvious. My state of mind is a medium through which the beauties of Paradise itself could not be communicated with any effect but a painful one. (Letter to Lady Hesketh, 13 October 1798)

For Hopkins, too, the awareness of inscape and the recognition of instress were barometers of spiritual health. His access to them was about to change dramatically.

In September 1873 he returned to Roehampton, to teach rhetoric for a year at Manresa House. It was an unhappy year. Even the secluded greenery of the gardens failed to compensate for a sense of failure and ineptitude as he struggled with the realisation that he was not a natural teacher. It was a year with some fruit to show at the end – he had taken the opportunity to visit galleries and museums in London, and had developed some ideas about poetic technique; all good preparation for what was to come. But Hopkins considered it his most depressing year so far.

The following August it was time to move again, this time to the Jesuit institution St Beuno's College, North Wales, where, as a Jesuit in training, he would go on to the next stage: three years studying theology. They were to be three of the happiest years of his life.

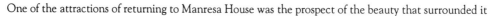
One of the attractions of returning to Manresa House was the prospect of the beauty that surrounded it

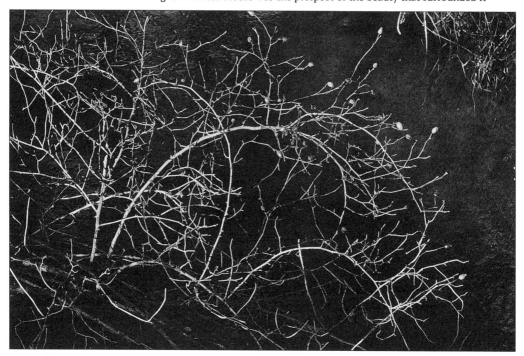

The original façade of Manresa House

The seclusion of Manresa House, that had been a confinement in the discipline of the novitiate, was a refreshing haven for Hopkins in one of his most exhausting years

St Beuno's

St Beuno's

There was a warm welcome for Hopkins when he arrived at St Beuno's. His heart must have already lifted as he approached Mynefyr Hill, with its views over the valley of the Clwyd; a gentle landscape, where farmers tended the land and fed their flocks as they had done for countless generations. St Beuno's is a building that can seem sometimes cold and severe, sometimes warm and comfortable: in winter its angled gables, four-square tower and sharp cornices stand out against the leafless skies; at other seasons the surrounding gardens lend a sympathetic beauty to the old building.

It was not an old building when Hopkins arrived there. His rooms were in the newly built wing that had increased the student capacity of the College, not before time; new rooms were being squeezed into all available spaces. By 1874 there were 173 priests and 139 'scholastics' at St Beuno's, and Hopkins was one of 14 first-year students out of a student body of 38. 'They were all of much the same age, had undergone the same formation and had the same purpose, to equip themselves as priests of the Society,' writes Paul Edwards in *Canute's Tower: St Beuno's* (1990). One of the new students was also called Hopkins: Frederick Hopkins, who later became Bishop of Honduras. He soon acquired the nickname 'the genteel Hop.'; Gerard was dubbed 'the gentle Hop.'

Hopkins tried his hand at learning Welsh, but gave it up on the advice of his instructor. He was fascinated by the language, and it certainly played a part in his later poetic development. There were other factors too. There were the journals and notebooks from the past few years, packed with observations and carefully crafted phrases, drawings and notes for drawings – materials ripe to be developed into poems, a temptation that Gerard was still resolutely rejecting. He had also discovered the previous year that his friend Robert Bridges, whose dislike of the Jesuits had not caused an irreparable breach between them, was a poet, which he had not realised before.

All these factors and more might have led him to contemplate resuming poetry at some stage. As we have seen, abstinence in this area was not a condition of membership of the Society, and one of his reasons for joining had been that he was fairly certain that his superiors would not forbid him to write. It might have happened, especially in the warm and supportive atmosphere of St Beuno's, that he would have re-thought his decision to abstain from poetry and approached his superiors for permission to write again.

As events turned out, the decision was taken out of his hands.

Opposite: well-head, Fynnon Fair. Hopkins was fascinated by the local wells

Below: Canute's Tower, St Beuno's

Away in the lovable west,
On a pastoral forehead in Wales,
I was under a roof here, I was at rest.
And they the prey of the gales;
She to the black-about air, to the breaker,
the thickly
Falling flakes, to the throng that catches
and quails
Was calling 'O Christ, Christ, come quickly':
The cross to her she calls Christ to her,
christens her wild-worst Best.

'The Wreck of
the Deutschland'

'The Wreck of the Deutschland'

The news of the death by shipwreck of five Franciscan nuns, bound for England after being exiled from Germany, reached St Beuno's in December 1875. The ship had foundered off the Kentish coast in a snowstorm and had broken up with terrible loss of life.

It was a tragedy that profoundly affected the 31-year-old Hopkins. The news reports were unsparing in their detail. *The Times* commented on 11 December,

> It is sad to know that these 200 fellow-creatures remained for some 30 hours so close to the English coast, passed by English vessels during the day, and their signals of distress seen and answered from the land at night, and that notwithstanding so many of them perished at the last.

Hopkins shared his distress with Fr Jones, the rector of St Beuno's. 'Somebody ought to write a poem about it,' the rector remarked, and thereby became responsible for many of the twentieth century's most original poems. For it was that remark which prompted Hopkins to write poetry again, and to resume a poetic body of work that would have an influence far beyond the tiny audience that read it in his lifetime.

'The Wreck of the Deutschland' is a very long poem, and for that reason is not included in the present book apart from some representative stanzas. However, it is a very important poem in Hopkins's output, not only for its position as the first of his mature poems, but also because it is the first fully-fledged example of 'sprung rhythm'.

Sprung Rhythm

Robert Bridges was dismayed when he first read 'The Wreck of the Deutschland', and advised readers to treat it with caution.

> The poem stands logically as well as chronologically in the front of his book, like a great dragon folded in the gate to forbid all entrance ... This editor advises the reader to circumvent him and attack him later in the rear; for he was himself shamefully worsted in a brave frontal assault, the more easily perhaps because both subject and treatment were distasteful to him.

And indeed, by comparison with Wordsworth, Tennyson, Byron or any other poet who writes in recognisable rhythms, Hopkins often seems impossible to follow on the page and even more so to read aloud. The biggest problem often seems to be how to fit all the words in, and which words to give the emphasis to. But once one understands his very personal use of rhythm and metre, it all becomes much easier.

Hopkins based his sprung rhythm on patterns of stressed words rather than

Lecture notes: an example of Hopkins's careful analysis of metre and the metrical accent markings he employed

metrical syllables. In a Hopkins line, several key words are the ones to emphasise, and the others (which he called 'hangers' or 'outriders') are to be fitted in once the stressed words have given the line its rhythm. He called this 'sprung rhythm', as opposed to the more usual 'running rhythm'. So in the first two lines of 'The

Windhover', the stresses fall as follows:

> I **caught** this **morn**ing **morn**ing's minion, **king-**
> dom of **day**light's **dau**phin, dapple-**dawn**-drawn **Fal**con,
>   in his **rid**ing ...

If you read the lines aloud, emphasising the stresses as marked, you will see that the five-stress pattern imposes its own unity and shape to the poem.

Hopkins believed he was recovering some of the virtues of Old English poetry, and much of his poetry has the same sinewy strength and vigour as the Anglo-Saxons achieved (if you are familiar with the Church of England liturgy and 'pointing', you will recognise a similar technique). But much more importantly, his distinctive style reinforces his distinctive choice of words. The breaking of the word 'kingdom', so ugly to the eye at first, drags the reader on to the next line. But by putting '-dom' on its own Hopkins connects 'kingdom' powerfully to the sequence 'daylight's dauphin, dapple-dawn-drawn Falcon'. And the stress on 'dawn' makes the complicated word-combination easier to understand: this falcon is drawn by the dappled dawn.

Much has been made of this technique, but it is not really original with Hopkins, any more than the notion of 'inscape' and 'instress' are unique to him (though known by other names in other places). It has much in common with Welsh poetry and with Hebrew poetry. It is almost disfigured with accents and stress marks, quite a few of which are not necessary as the underlying pattern of the verse is frequently clear enough not to need them. 'The Wreck of the Deutschland' is a good example; once you have grasped the number of strong stresses in each line, the rhythm draws you into the poem. (The stress pattern is: Part I, 2-3-4-3-5-5-4-6, and Part II the same, except that the first line has three stresses.) There are no 'outriders' to complicate matters and scanning the poem is simply a matter of allocating the right emphasis to the right words.

Read as he intended, Hopkins's individual and unfamiliar poetic forms make his poetry easier, not harder, and will give you a much deeper understanding of the meaning of some of his more unusual word-coinage.

A Synopsis of 'The Wreck of the Deutschland'

In *Mastery and Mercy: A Study of Two Religious Poems* (1957), Philip Martin points out that a comparison between the highly detailed, fact-filled accounts of the tragedy in the newspapers, and the poem that Hopkins wrote, tells us a great deal about poetry. Hopkins was not interested in creating a versification of the news narratives. He intended to produce a religious ode, that would set the tragedy and his own reaction to it into a much wider context. 'It has been said', writes Martin, 'that the best preparation for understanding "The Wreck of the Deutschland" is to meditate for a fortnight on the Passion of Christ.'

Statue in the grounds of St Beuno's.
In 'The Wreck of the Deutschland' Hopkins compares his
own spiritual security in the peaceful Welsh countryside,
with the faith and endurance of the doomed nuns in their sinking ship

Part I: Stanzas 1 to 10

The poet is prompted by the tragedy of the Deutschland to reflect upon his own dealings with God, on the divine mastery and mercy, and his own coming to God. Example stanza:

1

Thou mastering me
God! giver of breath and bread;
World's strand, sway of the sea;
Lord of living and dead;
Thou hast bound bones and veins in me, fastened me flesh,
And after it almost unmade, what with dread,
Thy doing: and dost thou touch me afresh?
Over again I feel thy finger and find thee.

Part II: Stanzas 11 to 23

Now he turns to consider God's initiative, and not merely in church but at sea, in the very plight of the five nuns. Here he tells the story of the wreck, but lifts it far beyond narrative. The events of the storm represent God's intervention, turning extreme suffering into God's mercy. Example stanza:

19

Sister, a sister calling
A master, her master and mine! –
And the inboard seas run swirling and hawling;
The rash smart sloggering brine
Blinds her; but she that weather sees one thing, one;
Has one fetch in her: she rears herself to divine
Ears, and the call of the tall nun
To the men in the tops and the tackle rode over the storm's brawling.

Stanzas 24 to 31

The poet considers the example of the heroic nun who faced death with obedience. While Hopkins experienced the grace of God in St Beuno's, God's incarnate grace and mastery was being experienced by the nun, whose weakness in the storm was offered to God. Example stanza: see stanza on p. 55, and also

30

Jesu, heart's light,

Jesu, maid's son,

What was the feast followed the night

Thou hadst glory of this nun? –

Feast of the one woman without stain.

For so conceivèd, so to conceive thee is done;

But here was heart-throe, birth of a brain,

Word, that heard and kept thee and uttered thee outright.

Stanzas 32 to 35

The poet concludes in praise to God, and adoration of Christ. Example stanza:

35

Dame, at our door

Drowned, and among our shoals,

Remember us in the roads, the heaven-haven of the Reward:

Our King back, oh, upon English souls!

Let him easter in us, be a dayspring to the dimness of us, be

a crimson-cresseted east,

More brightening her, rare-dear Britain, as his reign rolls,

Pride, rose, prince, hero of us, high-priest,

Our hearts' charity's hearth's fire, our thoughts' chivalry's throng's Lord.

Moonrise

I awoke in the Midsummer not-to-call night, | in the white and
    the walk of the morning:
The moon, dwindled and thinned to the fringe | of a finger-nail held to the candle,
Or paring of paradisaïcal fruit, | lovely in waning but lustreless,
Stepped from the stool, drew back from the barrow, | of dark Maenefa
    the mountain;
A cusp still clasped him, a fluke yet fanged him, | entangled him, not quit utterly.
This was the prized, the desirable sight, | unsought, presented so easily,
Parted me leaf and leaf, divided me, | eyelid and eyelid of slumber.

The caesuras (vertical bars) are an aid to reading and indicate a division of the line into two rhythmic units.
Paring of paradisaïcal fruit   A lovely image: light passing through semi-transparent peel of the fruit is like the light of the rising moon
Maenefa (Mynefyr)   The hill on which St Beuno's stands. This reference has made it possible to identify the part of the house in which Hopkins had his room; the description given pins it down to one of the three windows in the photograph on the facing page.
Cusp   The meeting of two curves.
Fluke   Here, the point of an anchor; there is also a sense of fins, as in the tail of a whale.
Fanged   The fluke, catching the moon; the anchor is perhaps personified as a beast holding the moon back with its teeth.

The St Beuno Poems

The writing of 'The Wreck of the Deutschland' released a flood of poetry. It was slow in gathering momentum; the poems of 1876 are insubstantial, including the fragment 'Moonrise'. We have included 'Moonrise' in this book mainly because it illustrates the precision of Hopkins's observation – so precise, in fact, that if you visit St Beuno's today they will show you the only two or three windows from which the view Hopkins describes could be seen. One of them, therefore, must have been the window of Hopkins's room.

The fragment occupies an interesting position in Hopkins's work. Not yet characteristic of the mature poetry that was soon to come, and not at all to be compared with the masterpiece of 1875 that had broken his self-imposed seven-year silence, it does indicate to some extent the movement away from his early poetry that had been taking place in Hopkins's thinking. The early poetry had mostly been painterly, surveying rather than engaging with the subject; brilliantly observed with almost physical descriptions of sense-experience, it remained somewhat detached from what it described. The conspicuous presence of the poet in his own poem that had been so central to the 'The Wreck of the Deutschland' is a far cry from the elegant, gifted observer recording with classical detachment a scene before him. Even in a confessional poem such as 'Heaven-Haven' (p. 10), we learn of the poet's desire to escape storms and hail, but very little

about storms and hail. The early Hopkins was a cross between an ascetic, and a writer of lush (and beautiful) verse influenced by Keats, Tennyson and Rossetti.

But even in the 'Moonrise' fragment we can detect a new voice. There is an identification with the moon, an acknowledgement of its plight, dragged by the hooked anchors of the woods on 'Maenefa' mountain. For Hopkins, the sight of the moon rising was a precious experience, 'the desirable sight'; now he had seen it by chance, without asking or planning. The moon is described in brief images of wasting (it is 'lustreless', it is 'dwindled', it is not even supreme in the skies, for being midsummer it is a 'not-to-call-night'), and some danger in the images of hooks and snares. But for the poet it is a blessing.

The few lines of the fragment do not in fact record an observation in which the observer confronts an object, from which he is detached apart from visual impressions. There is an exchange going on, a form of blessing; the sight of the moon, it may be, is an act of divine gratuitous grace ('unsought').

It *is* merely a fragment, and lacks the tightly composed inscapes of the later poems. But it does indicate that the new Hopkins is alive to the immanence of beauty, that there is more to the created world than beauty of design. From now on Hopkins was in the business of un-making appearances, of forcing the reader to look at familiar things as if they were quite new, and then making us look twice at what we would normally look past. The 'Moonrise' fragment was a clue to what would come later. What would come later would take him much farther.

God's Grandeur

The world is charged with the grandeur of God.
   It will flame out, like shining from shook foil;
   It gathers to a greatness, like the ooze of oil
Crushed. Why do men then now not reck his rod?
Generations have trod, have trod, have trod;
   And all is seared with trade; bleared, smeared with toil;
   And wears man's smudge and shares man's smell: the soil
Is bare now, nor can foot feel, being shod.

And for all this, nature is never spent;
   There lives the dearest freshness deep down things;
And though the last lights off the black West went
   Oh, morning, at the brown brink eastward, springs –
Because the Holy Ghost over the bent
   World broods with warm breast and with ah! bright wings.

Charged As a firearm is charged, or = 'intense', but perhaps also with the sense of given a responsibility: cf. Psalm 19:1-6.
Ooze of oil The seeping of oil from a press.
Reck Pay heed to.
Black West Note the observation that the horizon after sunset is black, and before sunrise is brown, tinged with the rising sun's rays.
Bent Carries the meaning of the curve of the earth (= the comprehensiveness of the Holy Spirit's presence) and bent = marred and spoiled, referring to the Fall.

'Over the Bent World'
God's Grandeur

> I mean foil in its sense of leaf or tinsel, and no other word whatever will give the effect I want. Shaken goldfoil gives off broad glares like sheet lightning and also, and this is true of nothing else, owing to its zigzag dents and creasings and network of small many cornered facets, a sort of fork lightning too.

Hopkins wrote the above to Robert Bridges, who found the opening of the poem difficult. But reading is helped by the very clear structure. This is a sonnet, a form that Hopkins was to make his own. The standard sonnet (and this is a standard sonnet) has fourteen lines, dividing into an 'octet' and a closing 'sestet'. The rhyme scheme varies, but the one Hopkins employs here is perfectly normal.

Hopkins's octet here has two parts. The first is a dazzling (literally!) evocation of the energy and power of God in nature. He uses images of power, electric and oil-fired; and the rhythm skilfully lets us down with a thud on the word 'crushed'. That word is expounded in the next four lines, where the multiplicity of verbs – nineteen different ones – in the first four lines gives way to the dreary repetition and monosyllabic inevitability of the four lines that talk of toil. Even the work man does has no profit, these lines seem to say, Ecclesiastes-like: the shoe that human labour makes and which protects the foot also removes the physical contact between human beings and the created world.

After that stark contrast between the energy of God and the exhaustion of the human lot, the sestet provides a benediction, full of images of repose and caring. The poem ends affirming that God is active in his creation, brooding over it; and that the resources of grace and providence are bottomless despite the reckless display of energy evoked in the opening lines. No wonder that the poet cannot quite get to the end of the poem before an involuntary exclamation escapes him:

> ... The Holy Ghost over the bent
> World broods with warm breast and with ah! bright wings.

The tide that ramps against the shore ...
'The Sea and the Skylark'

Difficult Expression
The Sea and the Skylark

Hopkins found the next sonnet difficult to write, and the reader is likely to find at least two difficulties in first reading it: the compressed language, and the imagery.

The compression looks strange at first sight, but is not a major barrier to enjoyment or understanding. Hopkins was unwilling to allow any word into his poems that did not earn its place, and he rejected many pronouns and other words. However, like most of Hopkins's difficult constructions, these lines become easier if read aloud, especially if you observe his metrical intentions.

He wrote to Bridges, who had expressed some concern over the difficult imagery. By now Bridges was a regular correspondent, an invaluable critic who did not let friendship blind him to any faults he considered the poems might possess. He provided explanations of some of the more difficult images; for example:

> Lines 6-7 ... a headlong and exciting (*rash-fresh*) new snatch of singing, resumption by the lark of his song, which by turns he gives over and takes up again (*re-winded*) all day long ...'

> Line 6 ... *new skeinèd score.* The lark's song, which from his height gives the impression ... of something falling to the earth and not vertically quite but tricklingly or wavingly, something as a skein of silk ribbed by having been tightly wound on a narrow card ...

The poem was written during a period when Hopkins was fascinated by a Welsh metrical device that he referred to as '*cynghanedd* or consonant-chime'. This was a complicated technique, using alliteration (words that begin with the same letter or sound) and internal rhymes. The dropped pronouns are also, (like the 'ah!' of the last line of 'God's Grandeur') characteristic of Welsh poetry.

The Sea and the Skylark

On ear and ear two noises too old to end
    Trench – right, the tide that ramps against the shore;
    With a flood or a fall, low lull-off or all roar,
Frequenting there while moon shall wear and wend.

Left hand, off land, I hear the lark ascend,
    His rash-fresh re-winded new-skeinèd score
    In crisps of curl off wild winch whirl, and pour
And pelt music, till none's to spill nor spend.

How these two shame this shallow and frail town!
    How ring right out our sordid turbid time,
Being pure! We, life's pride and cared-for crown,

Have lost that cheer and charm of earth's past prime:
    Our make and making break, are breaking, down
To man's last dust, drain fast towards man's first slime.

Trench Make an impression, as in a scored line or a trench. Hopkins is fond of using nouns as verbs.
Flood/fall High/low tide.
The town in line 9 is Rhyl in North Wales.

Make Breed, race, species.
Dust/slime Theological evocations of humanity's origins.

Also see opposite.

I remember a house where all
were good to me ...
'In the Valley of the Elwy'

In the Valley of the Elwy

I remember a house where all were good
   To me, God knows, deserving no such thing:
   Comforting smell breathed at very entering,
Fetched fresh, as I suppose, off some sweet wood.
That cordial air made those kind people a hood
   All over, as a bevy of eggs the mothering wing
   Will, or mild nights the new morsels of spring:
Why, it seemed of course; seemed of right it should.

Lovely the woods, waters, meadows, combes, vales,
All the air things wear that build this world of Wales;
   Only the inmate does not correspond:
God, lover of souls, swaying considerate scales,
Complete thy creature dear O where it fails,
   Being mighty a master, being a father and fond.

Inmate Of the house.
Correspond Combines 'respond' and
'correspond to' (the beauty of the landscape).

'All the Air Things Wear'
In the Valley of the Elwy

From the beginning of Hopkins's three years in Wales he was seized with a deep concern for the spiritual well-being of the people of the country he loved. That was one of the main reasons he decided to learn Welsh. The Jesuits are a strongly missionary society, and that aspect of their work had always appealed to Hopkins. But at St Beuno's he appears to have been gripped by a missionary vocation, which physical frailty and the assessment his superiors made of his gifts in that area prevented him from following as he may have wished. His notebooks are full of expressions of concern for the local people, and he never lost that concern.

'In the Valley of the Elwy' is, Hopkins confessed, not about the Elwy at all, but about 'the Watsons of Shooter's Hill'. The linking of two separate things – a place he loved and a home that had been hospitable – gives the poem a universality that is intentional, rather than it being a record of a single unique time and place.

Certainly the theme is universal. The house that was so welcoming – its fragrant wood fire, the shelter the house and its residents provided – is not the lovely pastoral image it might seem on a first reading. There is a terrible irony in this sonnet, revealed in the sestet. The people in the house, kind and welcoming though they be, are in dire spiritual need. Surrounded by the beautiful countryside of Wales they remain spiritually unmoved by it themselves: 'Only the inmate does not correspond.'

As we have seen already in the case of William Cowper, and as is the case with Wordsworth and many other poets of the period, failure to appreciate nature spiritually is a mark of spiritual problems. That explains the passionate appeal to God in the final three lines – an appeal based on the fatherhood of God (cf. the images of motherhood in the octet), that he will 'complete his creature', out of his love for 'souls'. What begins as a domestic and pastoral idyll ends as a desperate prayer of intercession.

'All Things Counter'
Pied Beauty

The next poem, 'Pied Beauty', is a 'curtal sonnet' – six lines followed by four, with a two-stress last line. The use of the latter as an exhortation to praise is a reminder that Hebrew verse, as in the psalms, is one of the influences on Hopkins's style.

This is indeed a psalm; a summer psalm. The opening sestet is full of images of the variegated beauty of nature, the colours of fishes' scales, birds' wings, flowers and growing things, using rich vocabulary and fresh word-coinages (for example 'couple-colour') that in their excitement almost commit acts of violence against the language. The riot of colour and variation is kept in balance by the poise of the verse itself, with a perfect rhythmic balance in the long line 5 – alliteration plays a part in avoiding total anarchy, too.

Nature is not a passive spectacle to be watched in all this. There is an energy in the variety. Nature praises God by simply *being* nature, in all its created richness. The sestet is a collection of inscapes, and the movement of the poem is instress – the poet, recognising the individual quality of each thing (even of individual trades and their trappings), recognises the hand of God, the universal source, the unchanged Beauty who created all the local beauties being described.

In the quartet, the poet seems to be doling out adjectives as if counting coins in a treasury. Each word adds to the picture of unity in diversity, of wondrous diversification, until in the last line of the quartet, and in the final line of the sonnet, he gives due praise to the Source of it all and brings his celebration to a satisfying, if reluctant, close.

An interesting aspect of this poem is that in previous centuries, variation in nature was sometimes seen as a sign of the Fall. For example the tulip, when first imported into England, was seen as a freak, endlessly fascinating to many poets for the variations in its colouring. Hopkins has no truck with such theories. He sees all diversity and variety in nature, however unrestrained and unorthodox, as coming from the hand of the Creator.

Pied Beauty

Glory be to God for dappled things –
   For skies of couple-colour as a brinded cow;
     For rose-moles all in stipple upon trout that swim;
Fresh-firecoal chestnut-falls; finches' wings;
   Landscape plotted and pieced – fold, fallow, and plough;
   And áll trádes, their gear and tackle and trim.

All things counter, original, spare, strange;
   Whatever is fickle, freckled (who knows how?)
     With swift, slow; sweet, sour; adazzle, dim;
He fathers-forth whose beauty is past change:
   Praise him.

Much of the unfamiliar in this sonnet does not
need a dictionary but simply the application of
the imagination. 'Fathers-forth', for example, is
quite clear from the context.
Counter Counter to the normal.
Spare = Sparse, without frills.

Freckled As noted earlier, variegation was
sometimes seen as fallenness, and the use of
'freckles' may be a corrective to that here.

Opposite: leaves dappling an abandoned truck
on army ranges, Bordon, Hampshire

Hurrahing in Harvest

Hop harvest, Selborne, Hampshire

'Half an hour of extreme enthusiasm ...'
Hurrahing in Harvest

Unlike 'In the Valley of the Elwy', this sonnet really is about the Valley of the Elwy! Composed on the first day of September 1877 while walking back to St Beuno's after a fishing expedition, it is another poem of celebration.

John Pick, in *Gerard Manley Hopkins: Priest and Poet* (1966 edn), writes,

> 'Pied Beauty' and the other poems of this group – indeed all that Hopkins ever wrote – are the poet's *Laudate Dominum* in which he calls on all creation to praise their Creator; for, as Peter the Venerable said, when the world ceases to offer sacrifice to God, it will cease to be God's.

The poem portrays a mood touching upon spiritual ecstasy. Later he tried to set the words to music, but the ecstasy belongs to the moment of writing the poem and is preserved in it. Like 'Pied Beauty', this sonnet collects images of inscape in its opening lines, but expressed as personal exclamations, direct responses by the poet to what he sees all around him. It is a dangerous beauty; the stooks are 'barbarous', the clouds are wilful and mouldering.

The young Hopkins would never have introduced himself so wholly into the poem as does Hopkins in the second half of the octet. The poet has a history in his own poem; he measures the moment's ecstasy against previous experience: 'What lips yet gave you a/Rapturous love's greeting of realer, of rounder replies?' Even the reckless run-on rhyme with 'Saviour' in the previous line merely adds to the sense of exaltation.

In the sestet, like a good preacher, he turns to application, explaining the theological foundation for the experiences of the octet. It is necessary, but difficult; by the time Hopkins reaches his final line, he is lost in wonder and excitement all over again, and it becomes evident that the theology and the ecstasy are two sides of one and the same coin.

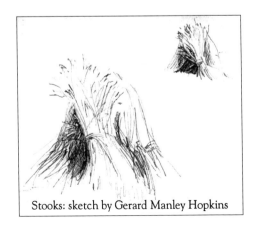

Stooks: sketch by Gerard Manley Hopkins

Hurrahing in Harvest

Summer ends now; now, barbarous in beauty, the stooks arise
  Around; up above, what wind-walks! what lovely behaviour
  Of silk-sack clouds! has wilder, wilful-wavier
Meal-drift moulded ever and melted across skies?

I walk, I lift up, I lift up heart, eyes,
  Down all that glory in the heavens to glean our Saviour;
  And, éyes, heárt, what looks, what lips yet gave you a
Rapturous love's greeting of realer, of rounder replies?

And the azurous hung hills are his world-wielding shoulder
  Majestic – as a stallion stalwart, very-violet-sweet! –
These things, these things were here and but the beholder
  Wanting; which two when they once meet,
The heart rears wings bold and bolder
  And hurls for him, O half hurls earth for him off
    under his feet.

Wind-walks Note Hopkins's fascination with
clouds, both as an artist and as a poet

(see also 'That Nature is a Heraclitean Fire',
p. 161).

'As kingfishers catch fire, dragonflies draw flame ...'

Creation's Praise
'As kingfishers catch fire ...'

Of all Hopkins's St Beuno's poems, this sonnet is the fullest exposition of the Christian creed that the chief duty of nature, as of human kind, is to glorify God and enjoy him for ever. The difference between them, as this sonnet explains, is that human beings have the capacity for conscious praise, by choice rather than by nature; as we have seen already, nature praises God simply by being nature; the glory of God is the trace of the maker's hand.

The poem is also an exposition of some key tenets of the teaching of Ignatius Loyola; the *Spiritual Exercises* are never far from Hopkins's poetry. The purpose of God in creation was that creation should glorify him, says Hopkins, repeating implicitly in this sonnet what he declared elsewhere in a famous sermon.

Again, the octet is a collection of inscapes, deliberately identified as such by the cry of 'each mortal thing': *What I do is me: for that I came* – a textbook definition, one might say, of Duns Scotus's doctrine of 'this-ness'. But the sestet brings the point home. Human beings are not mere created beauty. They are moral beings – 'The just man justices'. They bear the mark of the Creator – 'Christ plays in ten thousand places'. And – 'lovely in eyes not his' – they are redeemed.

'As kingfishers catch fire'

As kingfishers catch fire, dragonflies dráw fláme;
As tumbled over rim in roundy wells
Stones ring; like each tucked string tells, each hung bell's
Bow swung finds tongue to fling out broad its name;
Each mortal thing does one thing and the same:
Deals out that being indoors each one dwells;
Selves – goes itself; myself it speaks and spells,
Crying *Whát I do is me: for that I came.*

Í say móre: the just man justices;
Kéeps gráce: thát keeps all his goings graces;
Acts in God's eye what in God's eye he is –
Chríst – for Christ plays in ten thousand places,
Lovely in limbs, and lovely in eyes not his
To the Father through the features of men's faces.

Roundy wells The well at Manresa House was said to be the deepest in London and stones were dropped in it to demonstrate its depth. *Tucked* Coinage for 'plucked'.

Lines 9-10 Humans being made moral have the capacity to act accordingly; as the repository of God's grace, the Image-bearer of God, grace is available to them in all their doings.

'You cannot tell what a slavery of mind ... it is to live my life in a great town.'

Letter to Robert Bridges

Chesterfield, London, Oxford and Bedford Leigh

A Priest at Large

At the end of his time at St Beuno's Hopkins was ordained priest, in a festive ceremony that brought the years of study, devotions and poetry to an end in an appropriately joyous atmosphere. He did not have to wait long to find out his next step: in October he was sent to Mount St Mary's College in Chesterfield, where he found himself in the industrial Midlands. The change from the beloved landscape of Wales had predictable results; he disliked the new surroundings and once again suffered debilitating illness, this time chronic diarrhoea. It was half a year before he picked up his pen and wrote poetry. By then he had been transferred again, to a temporary teaching position at Stonyhurst. There, in March 1878, he began to write again, prompted by a similar tragedy to that which had prompted him before: the Eurydice, a training ship carrying young naval apprentices, was shipwrecked and lost at sea with great loss of life.

Hopkins sent a copy of the poem that he wrote about the wreck to Robert Bridges, who was no doubt pleased that Hopkins had chosen a less ambitious metrical scheme for the poem but was not overly impressed with it. Nevertheless it was now that he began systematically to preserve all the poems that Hopkins sent him; the fruit of this was the collected edition of 1918, which was the first published collection of Hopkins's poetry.

It was at this point in his life, too, that Hopkins began corresponding with somebody else who was to become extremely important in his life: Richard Dixon, who had taught Hopkins at Highgate. He was now, after a predicted brilliant career had failed to materialise, living a humdrum life as a vicar. Between the two a close friendship developed, though Dixon found it hard to understand Hopkins's reluctance to accept his offers to get his poems published.

From Stonyhurst he went, in July, to be temporary curate at Farm Street Church in London's fashionable Mayfair, and in December moved once more. This time he was sent to Oxford, to be Curate at the church of St Aloysius. In Oxford, scene of his academic triumphs, ecclesiastical struggles and early out-pouring of poetry, the doors of his imagination opened again. Between February and October of 1879 he wrote nine poems, and began to try his hand at composing music.

Inner-city Liverpool, 1970s:
women at a street-market stall

92

O if we but knew what we do
When we delve or hew –
Hack and rack the growing green!

'Binsey Poplars: felled 1879'

'Sweet especial rural scene'
Binsey Poplars

Hopkins had a particular fondness for trees. He had sketched many of them, and trees were an important part of many of his favourite landscapes, whether it be the mantled hills behind St Beuno's, the unspoilt commons of his childhood home at Hampstead, or the secluded walks and gardens of Manresa House. It was at Stonyhurst that the felling of a single tree had reduced him to bitter grief:

> I heard the sound and looking out and seeing it maimed there
> came at that moment a great pang and I wished to die and not
> see the inscapes of the world destroyed any more.

The occasion of 'Binsey Poplars' was the discovery, on a walk to Godstow, that the poplars lining the river at Binsey (a hamlet close to Oxford) had been cut down. He wrote an anguished note to Richard Dixon, and committed his deeper thoughts to paper in poetry.

There is little that needs explaining in the poem; grief seems to have lent simplicity to the style and the sadness is communicated by such devices as the repetition of 'felled' in line 3. It is worth looking particularly at the powerful image in the second stanza, where the loss of the trees is compared to being blinded by a small cut; a few poplars are of immense significance in the cosmic scale, for they represent inscape, the hand of God. By this image, too, Hopkins shifts the tragedy from the destruction of a landscape to the destruction of the possibility of observing and communicating. Hence it is not only a poem about the destruction of inscape, but of instress too; the poplars that have been felled were not just evidence of the creator, they were also access to him.

Binsey Poplars:
felled 1879

My aspens dear, whose airy cages quelled,
Quelled or quenched in leaves the leaping sun,
All felled, felled, are all felled;
   Of a fresh and following folded rank
      Not spared, not one
      That dandled a sandalled
   Shadow that swam or sank
On meadow and river and wind-wandering weed-winding bank.

O if we but knew what we do
     When we delve or hew--
  Hack and rack the growing green!
     Since country is so tender
  To touch, her being só slender,
  That, like this sleek and seeing ball
  But a prick will make no eye at all,
  Where we, even where we mean
     To mend her we end her,
  When we hew or delve:
After-comers cannot guess the beauty been.
   Ten or twelve, only ten or twelve
     Strokes of havoc únselve
     The sweet especial scene,
  Rural scene, a rural scene,
  Sweet especial rural scene.

Duns Scotus's Oxford

Towery city and branchy between towers;
Cuckoo-echoing, bell-swarmèd, lark-charmèd, rook-racked,
     river-rounded;
The dapple-eared lily below thee; that country and town did
Once encounter in, here coped and poisèd powers;

Thou hast a base and brickish skirt there, sours
That neighbour-nature thy grey beauty is grounded
Best in; graceless growth, thou hast confounded
Rural rural keeping – folk, flocks, and flowers.

Yet ah! this air I gather and I release
He lived on; these weeds and waters, these walls are what
He haunted who of all men most sways my spirits to peace;

Of realty the rarest-veinèd unraveller; a not
Rivalled insight, be rival Italy or Greece;
Who fired France for Mary without spot.

Opposite: library window, Balliol College

Keeping Harmonious balance.

Realty = Reality.
Rarest-veinèd As fine marble, with perhaps
the implication of coursing through the vein.

Duns Scotus's Oxford – and Hopkins's

At this time I had first begun to get hold of the copy of Scotus on the *Sentences* in the Baddely library and was flush with a new stroke of enthusiasm. It may come to nothing or it may be a mercy from God. But just then when I took in any inscape of the sky or sea I thought of Scotus. (Journal, 19 July 1872)

If Duns Scotus really did live and work in Oxford at the turn of the fourteenth century (and it is not certain that he did), it was a very different Oxford to that which Hopkins knew. Yet the picture one might receive from this poem – of an ancient city faced with a new

and destructive modernising challenge – is misleading. Oxford had been changing through the centuries long before Hopkins knew the city, and it has continued to change. The window in Balliol's Great Hall (p. 98) is a good example. In Duns Scotus's time the Hall had yet to acquire most of its splendid stained glass; and though Hopkins would have known the window, it would have been much more difficult to see it, as the Great Hall of his day was not, as it is now (in its new incarnation as the Library), divided into several storeys.

Scotus's 'towery city' had acquired a 'base and brickish skirt', a 'graceless growth'. It might seem that Hopkins, grieving the loss of an ideal city of learning and beauty, and mourning the spread of modern brick houses and industrial premises, occupied by people who had no idea who Duns Scotus was and could never hope to study him at

101

university – was being snobbish. But others shared his concern, such as William Morris; and Wordsworth too had bemoaned the arrival of the Rydal Railway in the Lake District, for it would enable people to enter the region without proper preparation, their sensibility untutored to receive the spiritual and artistic benefits of such a place.

Men like Gerard Manley Hopkins lived beauty passionately and let go of it with difficulty. It would need the kind of campaigning reformer who came later to demand a proper balance between making provision for the disadvantaged and those deprived of aesthetic and intellectual opportunities, and the preservation of Britain's cultural and environmental heritage. The issue remains unsolved today, so perhaps not too much blame should attach to Hopkins for expressing his distaste rather than coming up with a workable alternative.

Opposite: the pulpit at St Aloysius' Church, Oxford, from which Hopkins preached

Below: water meadows near Binsey, a favourite country walk even today

'*Morning, Midday, Evening ...*'

Sacrifice, Peace and a Wedding March

The next three poems are all from 1879 but have very different settings.

'Morning Midday and Evening Sacrifice' is a poem of pastoral homily, the preacher urging his hearers of whatever age to offer themselves to God. St Paul's teaching in the book of Romans clearly lies, at least in part, behind Hopkins's use of the word 'sacrifice' – 'I beseech you therefore, brethren, by the mercies of God, that ye present your bodies a living sacrifice, holy, acceptable unto God, which is your reasonable service' (Romans 12:1). This is Hopkins at his pastoral best, appealing to his congregation to offer to God all that is best in their lives. Some, as he himself had done, will have the dawning gifts and graces of youth to offer – a morning sacrifice; others in the maturity of mid-life will offer themselves in their prime; others, in the evening of their lives, will have mastery to offer in the very jaws of death. None have only second-best to offer; all life's stages bear fruit worth the offering.

'Peace', on one level, indicates the emotional vulnerability that Hopkins suffered throughout his adult life; not for the first time one is reminded of William Cowper, whose 'Sometimes a light surprises' is a similar thought to Hopkins's 'I yield you do come sometimes'. This poem stands at the least uncomfortable end of a line of despair at the other end of which are the late, 'terrible' sonnets that Hopkins was to write in Dublin. Nonetheless, the sonnet concludes with the assurance that the peace of God is a sovereign peace, sometimes hard to understand but always a manifestation of the goodness of God. At a more immediate level, the poem reflects his troubled state of mind as he prepared to leave Oxford the following day to work as a preacher in Bedford Leigh, in the north of England near Manchester.

Leigh was for Hopkins a place of appalling ugliness, 'the houses red, mean and two-storied'. Yet he was touched by the plight of the people and longed to give them spiritual comfort. 'The air is charged with smoke as well as damp,' he wrote to Robert Bridges, 'but the people are hearty.' It was for this that Hopkins had left 'towery Oxford'. Nevertheless, it was at Bedford Leigh that he wrote 'At the Wedding March', a poem of simple celebration that characteristically in its final stanza places the marriage of the church couple into the wider context of the Church as Bride of Christ.

Previous page: leek flower-heads

106

Morning Midday and Evening Sacrifice

The dappled die-away
Cheek and wimpled lip,
The gold-wisp, the airy-grey
Eye, all in fellowship –
This, all this beauty blooming,
This, all this freshness fuming,
Give God while worth consuming.

Both thought and thew now bolder
And told by Nature: Tower;
Head, heart, hand, heel, and shoulder
That beat and breathe in power –
This pride of prime's enjoyment
Take as for tool, not toy meant
And hold at Christ's employment.

The vault and scope and schooling
And mastery in the mind,
In silk-ash kept from cooling,
And ripest under rind –
What life half lifts the latch of,
What hell stalks towards the snatch of,
Your offering, with despatch, of!

Wimpled The comparison of a baby's puckered lips to the head-dress of a nun is brilliantly visual, and sets the tone for a poem that is particularly rich in imagery.
Fuming This neatly balances the idea of the boundless energy of youth with its transitoriness; fuming like smoke.
Thew A favourite word of Hopkins, it means 'strength'.
Toy A warning not to treat God's gifts as intended merely for selfish gratification.
Vault Evokes the dome of the (bald) skull.
Silk-ash Line 3 of the stanza is a very precise image of a wood fire cooling after a blaze.

The last three lines are in tightly compressed syntax, adding urgency to the appeal. The last line has the meaning 'This is your offering; make it as quickly as you can.'

Peace

When will you ever, Peace, wild wooddove, shy wings shut,
Your round me roaming end, and under be my boughs?
When, when, Peace, will you, Peace? I'll not play hypocrite
To own my heart: I yield you do come sometimes; but
That piecemeal peace is poor peace. What pure peace allows
Alarms of wars, the daunting wars, the death of it?

O surely, reaving Peace, my Lord should leave in lieu
Some good! And so he does leave Patience exquisite,
That plumes to Peace thereafter. And when Peace here does house
He comes with work to do, he does not come to coo,
    He comes to brood and sit.

Reaving An Old English word meaning 'to carry away by force'.

To coo Referring back to the opening dove image.

A Travelling Vocation

A modern Jesuit scholar at St Beuno's, Michael Ivens SJ, has written of Ignatius:

> As a teacher of prayer and contemplation, Ignatius is widely associated with an emphasis on methods. Undoubtedly, the methods expounded in the *Exercises*, especially the method by which the retreatant is initiated into the tradition of imaginative contemplation, have proved a significant contribution to post-Reformation spirituality. But the distinctive characteristic of his doctrine on prayer is not a concern with methods (which he regarded as important at the early stage of growth, but as constrictive later on), but a concern that prayer be integrated with service. ('Ignatius Loyola', in: C. Jones, G. Wainwright and E. Yarnold, *The Study of Spirituality* (SPCK, 1986), p. 362.

The influence of the *Exercises* can be seen in much of Hopkins's later writing and teaching. But Ignatius's other major work, the *Constitutions*, provided a further framework, illuminating, for example, the way his superiors moved him around so much. Michael Ivens writes of the *Constitutions*,

> The apostolic end of the Society is conceived in the widest possible terms: 'to labour for the defence and propagation of the Christian faith and the progress of souls', not only through preaching and the sacraments, but by 'any ministry of the word' and 'any work of charity' and this throughout the world ... The Constitutions insist, therefore, upon a high degree of mobility and an 'ordinary' external life-style. (p. 361)

It was for this reason as much as the needs of under-resourced Catholic communities scattered throughout Britain that Hopkins was able to write wryly to Mowbray Baillie, 'I have been long nowhere yet.' It was Jesuit mission strategy.

At the Wedding March

God with honour hang your head,
Groom, and grace you, bride, your bed
With lissome scions, sweet scions,
Out of hallowed bodies bred.

Each be other's comfort kind:
Déep, déeper than divined,
Divine charity, dear charity,
Fast you ever, fast bind.

Then let the March tread our ears:
I to him turn with tears
Who to wedlock, his wonder wedlock,
Déals tríumph and immortal years.

Lissome scions Agile, lithe children; a scion is a trimmed shoot of a plant intended for grafting; here meaning 'children'; Hopkins is alluding to the Catholic Mass.
I turn to him Hopkins uses the first person because he is no longer only talking about the couple. 'Him' is God, specifically Christ who, making the Church his bride, confers victory and eternal life through his death and resurrection.

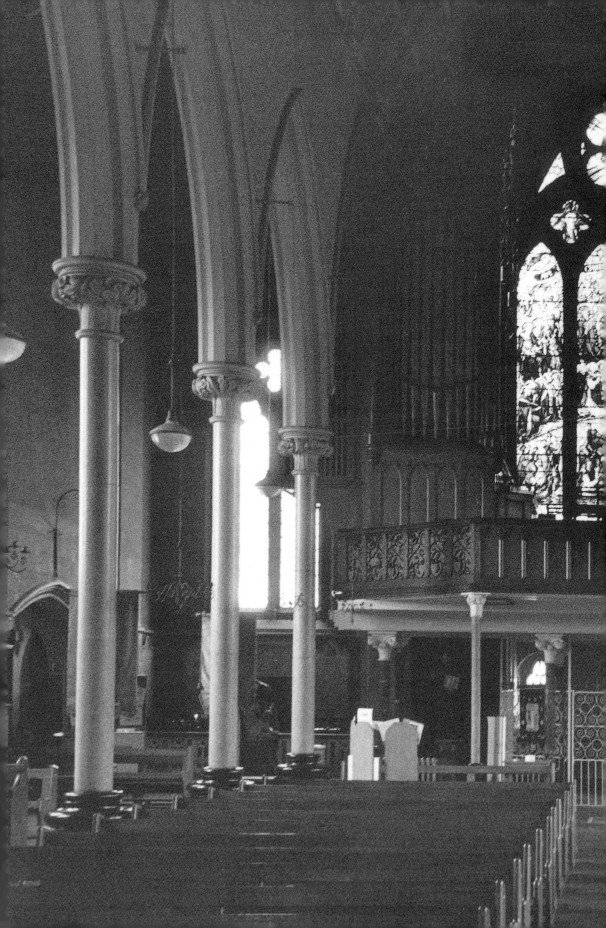

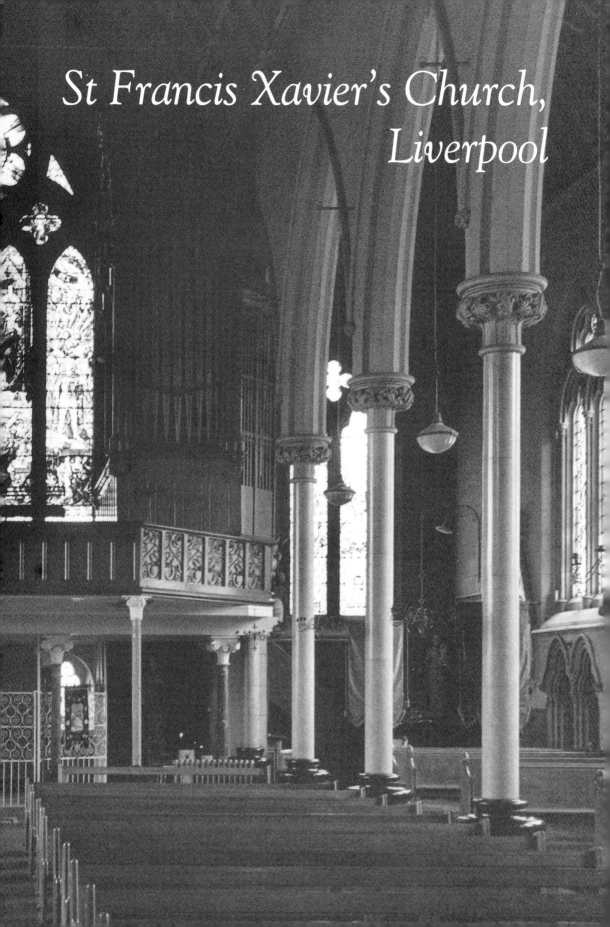

St Francis Xavier's Church, Liverpool

St Francis Xavier's Church survived the 1941 May Blitz that laid waste large tracts of central Liverpool. Today it stands in a network of narrow streets, not far from the Roman Catholic Cathedral of Christ the King. There are many similar buildings in the city centre, surrounded by faded tumble-down once-proud houses and boarded-up shops; churches like St Philip Neri, with its tangled ornamental garden that priests over the years have occasionally taken in hand; or the huge Catholic church a little further down the hill from St Francis Xavier's, surrounded by the wreckage of derelict buildings and neat rows of post-war semis with trim front privet hedges. The friendly verger will show you round the huge interior, kept bright and polished by a depressingly dwindling congregation who presumably simply do not have the resources to tackle the overgrown grounds that surround it within the high brick walls and ornamental gate that won't shut properly.

The area has never been prosperous. When in 1880 Hopkins came as a priest to Liverpool to care for a parish composed mainly of impoverished Irish residents, it was a slum. Today, years of economic depression and short-term housing development have left their own mark on the district. The wealthy merchants and professionals of the city, in Hopkins's day just as in ours, preferred the cleaner air of the inland parks and avenues, where the mansions they built are today mainly turned into flats. For Liverpudlians with the luxury of a choice, the lower ground nearer the river was a place to be avoided; poor diet and bad living conditions made the slums breeding grounds for virulent diseases of all kinds. Hopkins would certainly have had to minister to many sick parishioners.

One of them, it has recently been discovered, was the local farrier (a farrier is a shoer of horses) Felix Randal, who was the subject of one of the three poems we possess that are all we know Hopkins to have written in Liverpool.

The poem is intensely personal. For Hopkins, 1880 was a year of enormous spiritual and mental distress. He described himself, in a letter written that year, as 'so fagged, so harried and galled up and down'. In modern psychological terms he seems to have been ripe for a nervous breakdown.

Not for the first or last time in his life he found himself in an urban landscape bereft of the beauty that he loved and sought. He found himself temperamentally unsuited, too, for the more rigorous aspects of the Jesuit life, but was also awkward with his new parishioners. They were in turn perplexed as to what to make of the new priest and his scholarly sermons in which he heroically, and largely unsuccessfully, strove to express Catholic theology in terms that the uneducated layman could understand.

All of which makes the close relationship that appears to have grown up between Hopkins and the ailing, probably uneducated and certainly prickly character Felix Randal the farrier, an unlikely one. On the other hand, a letter of 22 May explains:

> With the Lancastrians ... I felt as if [I] had been born to deal with them. Religion, you know, enters very deep; in reality it is the deepest impression I have in speaking to people, that they are or that they are not of my religion. And then it is sweet to be a little flattered and I can truly say that except in the most transparently cringing way I never am. Now these Lancashire people of low degree or not of high degree are those who most have seemed to me to welcome me and make much of me ...

We do not know what disease killed Felix Randal, but it was clearly a wasting sickness that reduced this once physically impressive man to a shadow of his former strength. But parallel with the relentless processes of physical deterioration, Hopkins charts the spiritual transformation that has been taking place, in the opposite direction, in his parishioner's soul. Sickness and weakness are achieving reconciliation and serenity in this tempestuous man, of whose past abrasive character Hopkins gives us some hints.

The poem, too, reflects on the bond that develops between the priest and his charge; that there is a spiritual need that is satisfied by ministering to the needy. This is a poem in which neither party is presented as the emotional and spiritual core of the situation. Ultimately, priest and parishioner minister to each other.

Felix Randal

Felix Randal the farrier, O is he dead then? my duty all ended,
Who have watched his mould of man, big-boned and hardy-handsome
Pining, pining, till time when reason rambled in it and some
Fatal four disorders, fleshed there, all contended?

Sickness broke him. Impatient, he cursed at first, but mended
Being anointed and all; though a heavenlier heart began some
Months earlier, since I had our sweet reprieve and ransom
Tendered to him. Ah well, God rest him all road ever he offended!

This seeing the sick endears them to us, us too it endears.
My tongue had taught thee comfort, touch had quenched thy tears,
Thy tears that touched my heart, child, Felix, poor Felix Randal;

How far from then forethought of, all thy more boisterous years,
When thou at the random grim forge, powerful amidst peers,
Didst fettle for the great grey drayhorse his bright and battering sandal!

The Consolation of Friendship:
Felix Randal

With what tone of voice are we meant to read Hopkins's simple question: 'O is he dead then?' It could be the polite acknowledgement of news of an expected decease; it could be mild surprise that death has occurred perhaps sooner than anticipated. But, after reading the poem through, there can be no doubt that the words are an exclamation of sadness, blurting out the shock of personal loss.

For this is a poem about a close-knit relationship, the tight bond between counsellor and counselled, and a relationship that appears to have developed, at least on Hopkins's side, into heartfelt love. It is unnecessary to find, as some have done, a link between the poet's descriptions of the farrier's physical beauty and Hopkins's sexuality. One of the main emotions that drives the poem is the poet's familiar grief over physical decay of any kind, from the unleaving of Goldengrove (p. 125) and the felling of Binsey's poplars (p. 97), to the extremes of physical mortality as seen here in a strong man's body falling apart.

Alliteration plays an important part in the poem, even in Felix Randal's name which conveniently echoes his trade. Just as Hopkins and Randal are drawn into an entwined relationship of love through the administering of the comforts of religion on Hopkins's part and spiritual awakening on Randal's, so the poem's words are tightly pulled into relationship by the alliteration. So in the first line, the repeated 'f' of Felix and farrier is followed by the triple 'd' of dead, duty and ended – which three words could be said to sum up the poem.

Lines 2 to 4 enact in their structure what their words mean. The celebratory line 2, with strong metrical rhythm that no doubt echoed the farrier's hammer-strokes in his forge, gives way to the repeated 'pining', and there is a sense of disintegration underlined by the way the sense runs on into the fourth line which, slowed down by commas, has a dying fall of its own.

Hopkins goes on to describe the spiritual as well as the physical pathology of Randal's disease, in language that undergoes the same transformation as its subject: the angry hammer-blows of 'sickness broke him' and the tortuous 'impatient, he cursed at first', give way to the mellow, liquid 'anointed and all ... a heavenlier heart'; Hopkins even makes use of some Lancashire dialect, increasing the intimacy of the poem: 'Ah well, God rest him all road ever he offended!'

We are brought now to the core of the poem, located, probably deliberately, at line 9: this is a sonnet, and the ninth line of a sonnet traditionally introduces a shift of direction towards the poem's conclusion.

The Exchange of Love

Line 9 is typically ambiguous. What does Hopkins mean by the word 'endear'? On the simplest level it expresses succinctly the main point that Hopkins wants to make; that the shared experience of ministering and being ministered to has made both men more beloved in the eyes of the other. For Randal, Hopkins is the bearer of the 'sweet reprieve and ransom' of the Church; for Hopkins, Randal is explicit evidence of God's grace at work. But there is also the suggestion that the experience has increased the perceived worth of each; that the privilege of being a mediator of grace and sacrament has made Hopkins a person of greater worth in an absolute, objective sense; and seeing the transformation in Randal has made him of infinite value in the eyes of his priest, and of course in the eyes of God.

Gerard Manley Hopkins in 1880

But as we have seen, the transformation is two-way. Spiritual progress is matched by physical decline. Once it was the farrier who was physically strong, 'big-boned and hardy-handsome'; now it is Hopkins (whose photograph taken in the same year shows him as still a delicate, almost fragile individual) who must use his physical skills, his tongue bringing words of comfort, his touch physically drying Randal's tears, almost as a parent comforting a child. And that is what, the first stanza explains, Randal has become; his body broken by sickness, his reason too is rambling. Hence the caressing line 11 – 'child, Felix, poor Felix Randal' – as if Hopkins feels barely able to assume the privilege of first names, yet in the repeated naming seems to be recalling the man's baptism.

The last stanza is both an expression of grief, and an exhortation to Hopkins's readers. The brilliant declamatory celebration of the farrier's best years, laden with adjectives like 'boisterous', 'powerful', and 'bright', sets the farrier as regal in a 'grim' forge, where the 'great grey drayhorse' receives his 'bright and battering sandal' fashioned by Felix Randal's strong hands. A more dramatic contrast with the drawn shades and sombre voices of the sick room can hardly be imagined. Certainly it is a contrast that was 'far from then forethought of', so far as Felix Randal was concerned.

For Hopkins's readers, the warning is clear. 'Memento Mori' is the underlying message of this moving sonnet, and Hopkins's poignant eulogy for one who had clearly become a cherished companion acquires the force of an evangelistic tract.

119

Moving though Hopkins's poem on the death of Felix Randal is, it is no mere sentimental tribute. Visiting the sick, even entering their homes, was an act of courage in 1880 Liverpool, and priests and clergy were one of the few groups willing to do it.

Disease was rampant in Liverpool, with its large Irish population made up largely of those who had come as immigrants after the devastating potato famine of 1845-50. It had cost the lives of a million people and a further million had emigrated. Dysentery and typhus spread rapidly, carried by the sick and starving as they searched for food. Most of those who arrived in Liverpool were either physically weakened by famine and starvation, or were already carriers of virulent and infectious illness.

It was not long either since the cholera epidemic of 1865-66, the latest of several recent epidemics. Cholera, a disease of the intestines, was carried to Britain from India. It was an extremely contagious disease and was often fatal.

St Francis Xavier's today. Hopkins would recognise this room and much of the furnishing and fittings that remain

Below: the side entrance and its tiny courtyard. The drab stone edifices and poor houses of Liverpool depressed Hopkins, and left him starved of beauty

The authorities, who were not quick to act in this crisis, had realised belatedly that infected water supplies were the cause of the disease spreading so widely, and had recently passed the Sanitary Act in an attempt to halt the epidemic.

Social conditions helped the spread of the disease, but so did factors such as prostitution, a common element in Victorian society. The widespread incidence of sexually transmitted diseases had already prompted the Contagious Diseases Acts, which were couched in rhetoric but failed adequately to get to grips with the problem. Hopkins's Liverpool slum was not a healthy place, and by entering people's homes and tending them in their sickness he and his fellow-priests were running serious risks.

In Liverpool, Hopkins found a situation where beauty was largely absent and physical revulsion something that had to be faced as part of his daily work. According to Robert Bridges, the immorality and appalling suffering of the people almost killed the young Jesuit.

The churches staked out the territory for God when most people avoided the area fastidiously. The Jesuits were not the only Christians active there; for example Silas Hocking, an Evangelical religious novelist who lived in Liverpool for three years, wrote in 1879, in the preface to his novel *Her Benny*, of the destitute child street-traders of the city. They lived in streets a short walk from St Francis Xavier's:

> A regular network of streets, inhabited mostly by the lowest classes of the Liverpool poor. And those who have occasion to penetrate their dark and filthy recesses are generally thankful when they find themselves safe out again. In the winter those streets and courts are kept comparatively clean by the heavy rains; but in the summer the air fairly reeks with the stench of decayed fish, rotting vegetable, and every other conceivable kind of filth.

In this pulpit at St Francis Xavier's, Hopkins struggled to master the art of comprehensible preaching

It was a time and place where few lived healthily and most died before their time. For those of a religious disposition the next life was a more secure prospect than the present one. So it is not surprising to find the theme of mortality preoccupying Hopkins during his time at Liverpool, as for example in the following poem, 'Spring and Fall', written during a brief absence from the city.

Goldengrove unleaving ...

'Spring and Fall'

Sorrow's Springs:
Spring and Fall

Margaret in this poem is an imaginary child, and the poem is not (like 'Harry Ploughman') based on direct observation, nor is it (like 'The Wreck of the Deutschland') a response to contemporary events. This is an abstract meditation on the theme of mortality, couched in familiar Hopkins metaphors of loss, destruction and the despoiling of nature, in this case at nature's own hand.

The poet describes a young girl, moved to sorrow by the sight of the leaves in autumn falling from the trees (immediately we are presented with a triple word-play on 'fall' = autumn, 'fall' = the leaves' descent, and 'fall' = the theological term). He marvels that she is capable of responding so, and reminds her that with the passing of the years will come a hardening of the emotions and a loss of the ability to grieve for such things, even if whole worlds of leaves were falling.

Yet, he warns, she *will* weep then, and she will, unlike now, understand why. Whatever one chooses to call it, human sorrow ultimately all comes from one root; the original fall, the entry of death into human experience.

And from that, Hopkins concedes, there is no escaping. She may well weep for the unleaving of Goldengrove. For she is weeping for her own sure death sooner or later.

Though the poem has a strong pastoral feel, it is worth reminding ourselves that for many months the only children that Hopkins had had much to do with were slum children. It was to the slums he was returning when he composed the poem, on his way to the station after saying mass in a country church. The inevitability of mortality was much more easily recognised where life expectancy was short, the streets were dangerous, and dereliction and poverty were everywhere.

That is why the photograph overleaf translates these themes into a 1970s urban, inner-city Liverpool context.

Spring and Fall:
To a Young Child

Márgarét, áre you gríeving
Over Goldengrove unleaving?
Leáves, líke the things of man, you
With your fresh thoughts care for, can you?
Áh! ás the heart grows older
It will come to such sights colder
By and by, nor spare a sigh
Though worlds of wanwood leafmeal lie;
And yet you wíll weep and know why.
Now no matter, child, the name:
Sórrow's spríngs áre the same.
Nor mouth had, no nor mind, expressed
What heart heard of, ghost guessed:
It ís the blight man was born for,
It is Margaret you mourn for.

Inversnaid

This darksome burn, horseback brown,
His rollrock highroad roaring down,
In coop and in comb the fleece of his foam
Flutes and low to the lake falls home.

A windpuff-bonnet of fáwn-fróth
Turns and twindles over the broth
Of a pool so pitchblack, féll-fhrówning,
It rounds and rounds Despair to drowning.

Degged with dew, dappled with dew
Are the groins of the braes that the brook treads through,
Wiry heathpacks, flitches of fern,
And the beadbonny ash that sits over the burn.

What would the world be, once bereft
Of wet and of wildness? Let them be left,
O let them be left, wildness and wet;
Long live the weeds and the wilderness yet.

Hopkins was interested in how water behaves; much of the poem's vocabulary reflects this. *Coop* might refer to the recesses in which water collects and swirls. *Comb, Flutes* Both refer to the apparently solid ridges water makes as it pours over rocks. Hopkins drew this effect in his notebooks, and something of it can be seen in the photograph overleaf.

Twindles A Hopkins coinage, drawing on 'twine', 'twin', 'dwindle' and a number of other words. *Degged* A Lancashire dialect word meaning 'sprinkled'. *Heathpacks* A coinage from 'heath' = heather. *Flitches* A nineteenth-century word meaning strips of tree-trunk, here meaning the dried bracken fronds.

Glasgow

From August to October 1881 Hopkins was sent as assistant priest to St Joseph's Church, Glasgow, where he found himself once more working among Irish immigrants in a slum district. Once again he felt himself spiritually torn between revulsion for the squalid social conditions in which they lived and the moral degradation he saw around him – and his love for those same people, and the affection which seems to have been mutual. In both Liverpool and Glasgow he wryly accepted his congregation's frank assessment of his preaching gifts, and accepted with good grace that he was never likely to win the same place in people's hearts as the much-loved and revered Father Clare, the priest at St Francis Xavier's.

Hopkins's sermons were in fact often compelling, and ingenious in creative ways; the poet of 'The Wreck of the Deutschland' and 'Pied Beauty' was incapable of handling words without creating some beauty. But his poor delivery and tendency to academic complexity were a barrier to good communication. His congregations frequently fell asleep while he was preaching and were not afraid to let Hopkins know that they had done so. Even Hopkins's often brilliant analogies and a characteristic disinclination to conform (which once led to him being forbidden for a period to preach without showing his sermon to a superior) failed to seize their attention.

Inversnaid

While at Glasgow he visited Inversnaid on Loch Lomond, and wrote the poem of that name that is printed on the previous page. It was, he wrote to his friend

Mowbray Baillie, a response to 'a pensive or solemn beauty which left a deep impression on me'. It is a heartfelt plea for the preservation of nature's 'wildness', made all the sharper by the ugly wildness of the city with which he was all too familiar. The old delight in detail rekindles, as the freshly coined language is used to force the reader to re-think what is familiar and see it in a different way. On a temporary break from urban landscapes that have been ground into dreary uniformity and ugly decay by human failings, he delights in the 'wet and wildness', the weeds and the 'beadbonny ash'. In other writings, he commented on 'the decline of wild nature'; in 'Inversnaid', he pleads for its reprieve.

The Tertianship

After Glasgow, it was time to return to Manresa House for the next stage of his novitiate.

The Tertianship was a further commitment to the Jesuit vows of poverty, chastity and obedience. It involved extended meditation, and was in effect a ten-month retreat. The Jesuit constitution describes it as a necessary period when, having cultivated the intellect, it was time to examine the heart, to study spiritual things, to make progress towards a better knowledge of God.

1880 and 1881 had been thin years for poetry. If he wrote poetry at Manresa House during the ten months of his tertianship, none survives, though he did begin to make notes in preparation for a commentary on the *Spiritual Exercises* of Loyola. There were literary projects that were abandoned; the play, *St Winefred's Well*, was destined never to be completed, and a planned ode on the anniversary of the great English Jesuit, Edmund Campion, seems never to have been begun. On the other hand his musical interests had flourished.

He had hoped on his way south from Glasgow to meet with R. W. Dixon, but his plans were already subject to his superiors' approval and the meeting had to be cancelled. During the year, however, he was sent to help out at churches in the north of England and while there was able to visit him on a 'repose day'. It was their first meeting since Dixon had taught him at Highgate, though they had been corresponding since 1878. It was a high point of the year, and was followed several weeks later by a meeting between Hopkins, Bridges and Dixon at Manresa House. Both Bridges and Dixon, in their different ways, had been reluctant to encourage Hopkins in his desire to enter the Society of Jesus; but friendship had overcome their disagreements. Both urged him to publish his poems and to write more. For Hopkins, despite the fact that all his Jesuit poetry had arisen from a suggestion made by a superior to write about the wreck of the Deutschland, there was still an occasional nagging uncertainty as to whether he ought ever to have started writing again after burning his early poems.

That he continued to write was due in large measure to the encouragement of his friends. That he continued to write few poems is due partly to his heavy workload, and partly because he was once more on the move; this time, he was to return to Stonyhurst as a classics teacher.

In September 1882 Hopkins left Roehampton and took up residence at Stonyhurst College, where he had already studied at seminary and worked as temporary teacher coaching examination candidates. His task now was the preparation of the senior boys for Latin and Greek examination.

Stonyhurst is a bleakly imposing house set in some of the loveliest countryside in northern England. The college dates as a teaching body from Elizabethan times, when English Roman Catholics established a college of St Omer in Artois in Spain. After relocating to Belgium, the college eventually settled in Lancashire and changed its name.

Two aspects of Stonyhurst at least were profoundly satisfying to Hopkins. First, by the mid-Victorian period Stonyhurst was not only the focus of Jesuit life in England, it was situated in a part of the country where Catholicism was deeply rooted; Lancashire was soaked in the history of the church that Hopkins loved. Second, the house itself was gracious and very conducive to reflection, meditation, prayer and writing. The grounds were as pleasant to walk in as when Hopkins had first studied at seminary, and from the upper floors there were views of the distant hills. Sometimes he traversed the old stone corridors and climbed the spiral steps in the towers, emerging on to the flat rooftops where he sat for hours watching the sky and the landscape; he began to make careful observations and report them in letters to friends, even on occasion publishing letters in the magazine *Nature*, describing a rare view of the Northern Lights, or how the sunbeams seemed to radiate like the spokes of a great wheel at sunset.

The library at Stonyhurst was – and is – a venerable place, where ancient volumes and contemporary books co-exist in reading rooms, and books line study alcoves shelved from floor to ceiling. There was academic, aesthetic and spiritual stimulus at Stonyhurst. For the poet who had stoically endured the ugliness and sorrow of the slums it was a place of blessed and revivifying fulfilment, though there were troubling periods of despond- ency and mental tiredness. He embarked on writing projects, scholarly investigations of classical themes that interested

him. His musical interests continued; among his letters from Stonyhurst are letters of thanks to Bridges for sending him some anthems. The sense of humour that had characterised him at Highgate returned, and he even wrote comic verses to entertain his colleagues and his pupils. More serious poetry, too, began to form in his mind. When he had left Roehampton to go to Stonyhurst, the Provincial of the Jesuits encouraged him to go on writing, and at Stonyhurst he began to write again. His output was small; this was not one of the periods of intense creativity in his life. But he did write one of the most accomplished of all his poems, *The Leaden Echo and the Golden Echo*. This is too long to include in the present book, but is a virtuoso piece of sprung rhythm in which there is total mastery of the form. Some have seen in its unusually long lines and metrical power an influence of Walt Whitman, the American poet whom Hopkins greatly admired.

Some of the handful of poems that Hopkins wrote during this period at Stonyhurst were, like poems he wrote at other times there, expressions of Catholic theology, for example 'The Blessed Virgin compared to the air we breathe', a contribution to a college celebration of Mary. *The Leaden Echo and the Golden Echo* is taken from his incomplete *St Winefred's Well*.

At Stonyhurst he also met another man of letters who was to become a close friend: the distinguished poet Coventry Patmore, who came for a college speech day and struck up an immediate friendship with Hopkins, who admired Patmore's work. The distinguished visitor, who though himself a convert to Catholicism did not much care for priests, became in turn a great admirer of Hopkins's work. However, it was some time after his visit that he discovered, through Bridges and Dixon, that the young priest who had so admired his poetry was a poet himself. The great man appears to have submitted not only to the younger man's rigorous reading of his work, but also to a spiritual authority that he recognised in Hopkins.

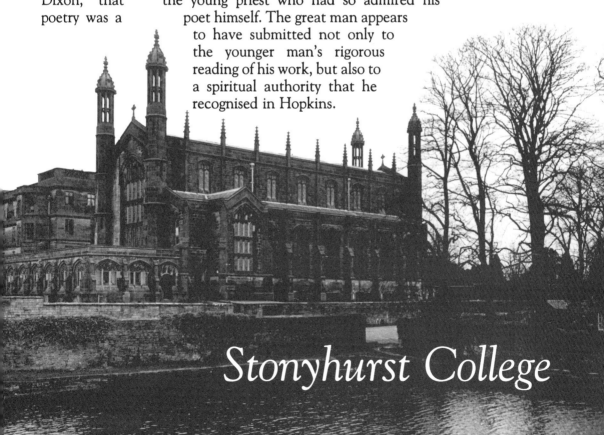

Stonyhurst College

Three views with which Hopkins was very familiar. Left, a typical study alcove in the college library, set up for reading just as it would have been set up in his day; below, a yew tree walk in the grounds, in which he loved to wander during each of his periods of residence at Stonyhurst; above, an observatory, one of the many small buildings that are to be found in the grounds.

There are acres of flat roof which, when the air is not thick, as unhappily it mostly is, commands a noble view of this Lancashire landscape, Pendle Hill, Ribblesdale, the fells, and all round, bleakish but solemn and beautiful. There is a garden with a bowling green, walled in by massive yew hedges, a bowered yew-walk, two real Queen Ann summerhouses, observatories under government, orchards, vineries, greenhouses, workshops, a plungebath, fivescourts, a mill, a farm, a fine cricketfield be-sides a huge playground ... (Letter to Robert Bridges)

Dublin

University College

In 1883 University College, Dublin, was placed under the management of the Jesuits. Seen as a vital educational counter-force in Ireland to the Protestant institutions, University College had been founded thirty years previously in association with the Royal University of Ireland. Newman had been its first rector, an unhappy experience for him, and subsequently the University had been in decline. Under the new president, Delaney, better things were hoped for. One of the first acts of the new governing body was to elect Hopkins as Professor of Greek and Latin Literature.

Within months of arriving in Dublin he was in severe depression. He arrived in February, and found a windy, cold and smoggy city and a badly equipped university. Even being in Ireland was mentally troubling; a committed patriot, he found himself being drawn into political stances and arguments. His new colleagues were academically strong, and Hopkins was pleased to find himself in stimulating academic company; but the library shelves were largely empty and his living quarters frugal. After the joys of an ancient well-filled library and extensive facilities at Stonyhurst, Dublin provided not so much a challenge as a mountain to climb.

It was a post that in the secular world would have been recognised as a promotion and an honour. The obscure schoolmaster at Stonyhurst had been chosen largely on the recommendation of Jowett, now Master of Balliol. Hopkins's immediate reaction to the news was that he would have rather been passed over and left where he was at Stonyhurst. He was daunted by the challenge of such a major geographical move, he felt physically too weak for the post, and he dreaded the mountain of marking he would have to do. His responsibilities included teaching and also examining for the Royal University, assessing the examination papers of hundreds of candidates.

His first task was to set the annual examination papers and mark the recent ones. He found the responsibility overwhelming, and went to extraordinary lengths to be fair in his marking. As a lecturer he had the same problems he had had as a preacher: learning and eloquence but a fundamental failure to communicate well. His students became bored and discipline was a problem.

His friends did not at first realise the problems brewing. Dixon, still a clergyman in lonely and difficult parishes, envied him the opportunity both to read and to teach and congratulated Hopkins on his professorship, which he regarded as a great distinction. In Dublin, Hopkins became something of a recluse, venturing rarely beyond the university environment, though paradoxically, among the few friends he made were several women – one a poetess; another, Miss Cassidy of nearby Monasterevan, was to become a good friend and confidante.

The entrance to University College, Dublin (now Newman House)

The Sonnets of Desolation

Over a year after arriving in Dublin, Hopkins wrote to Robert Bridges and told him that several sonnets had come 'like inspiration unbidden and against my will', and that he was sending them to him. In fact Bridges never received them, but from Hopkins's descriptions (for example, 'If ever anything was written in blood one of these was'), he was able to identify them with some confidence in the pile of manuscripts that were passed to him when Hopkins died.

There are around half a dozen sonnets. Two that follow in this book are almost certainly among them, and a third – 'Thou art indeed just, Lord' – is considered by some to be one of the group. The strong note of hope in that poem makes it somewhat different to the others, which are very dark poems indeed.

The sonnets are the work of a man who is intensely lonely, facing physical weakness and spiritual struggles. They are for Hopkins his 'dark night of the soul', and their depiction of states of mind when God seems absent or arbitrary are all the more searing in the context of the rest of his poetry, which celebrates so strongly the immanent omnipresence of God. In the 'terrible sonnets', inscape dies.

Opposite: a sheet of Hopkins's examination marks, showing his painstaking system of subdividing the marks to ensure fairness. A dramatic portrayal of a mind under terrible emotional stress, these sheets include poem fragments and other jottings, sometimes almost buried under the rows of ticks

Below: a lecture-room in Newman House today, preserved as it was when Hopkins taught there

What is it a lot of them mean by talking of "Tyndaris" or the
"Daughter of Tyndareus" when they std. say Helen plainly?

For when thy folding star a-ri— sing shows
re   do   re   mi   do (sf)mi mi do ti   la   ti do

His pa-ly circ-let, at his warn-ing lamp
la   so   la ti   ti doti do re   la ti

the fra—

that slept in flowers the day
re re mi do do re ti la la

And many a nymph who wreathes her   wreathes   her
mi re do re re re mi re mi redo mi ti la ti la   do ti mi ti la ti la

Crows with sedge
4 so   la ti do   ti la mi la so la so
And sheds the fresh-en-ing do ta mi ti la ti la ti la so fa la
re mi re mi do ta   dew and
remi re do ti   so
so la

'*To seem the stranger lies my lot, my life*
Among strangers.'

Hopkins's room in Dublin

I am in Ireland now...
('To seem the stranger ...')

If you want to understand the depth of depression that motivated this deeply stricken sonnet, compare the previous photograph of Hopkins's room in Ireland with the photograph of the Stonyhurst library (p. 134) or indeed with any of the St Beuno's illustrations (pp. 50ff). Though the Jesuits are not monks, the sparseness of his room at University College and the fact that he relatively infrequently went outside his teaching environment meant that he had exchanged a life of comfortable, if not extravagant, circumstances for yet another ugly urban environment. St Stephen's Green, a local landmark close by the university and Hopkins's lodgings, was wintry and bare when he arrived. Had he arrived in summer it would have softened the transition.

But he was more than aesthetically bereft. The moving stanzas enumerate the scale of loss. His family are strangers, certainly in the sense of church attachment, to him – the first is a particularly sad stanza when one remembers the childhood home life he had enjoyed. England, his ideal as a fervent nationalist, is deaf to him now that he is a bystander at conflicts and wars.

In stanza 3 he obliquely acknowledges that even in Ireland, there is much love to be found and to be given. But the only defence he has against heaven's 'baffling' silence or the machinations of hell is his poetry, which he is willing to 'hoard unheard'. But that is a lonely occupation ...

'To seem the stranger lies my lot'

To seem the stranger lies my lot, my life
Among strangers. Father and mother dear,
Brothers and sisters are in Christ not near
And he my peace/my parting, sword and strife.
   England, whose honour O all my heart woos, wife
To my creating thought, would neither hear
Me, were I pleading, plead nor do I: I wear-
y of idle a being but by where wars are rife.

   I am in Ireland now; now I am at a third
Remove. Not but in all removes I can
Kind love both give and get. Only what word
Wisest my heart breeds dark heaven's baffling ban
Bars or hell's spell thwarts. This to hoard unheard,
Heard unheeded, leaves me a lonely began.

Father and mother ... Brothers and sisters
Though High Anglican, Hopkins's family was
not Roman Catholic.
My peace/my parting A reference to Christ's
double claim to give his peace (= the Holy
Spirit) after leaving his disciples (John
14:15ff), and also to bring not peace but a
sword (Matthew 10:34). This paradox is
working out painfully in Hopkins's life. Note
the play on 'parting'.

England He finds it hard to live among
English people in Ireland who do not share his
nationalism.
Third remove The geographical removal, first
from home, then to the itinerant Jesuit
vocation, and now to a foreign country. The
spiritual alienations of his life are very much
included here.
Began A potential: a good start that has
faltered.

'No worst'

No worst, there is none. Pitched past pitch of grief,
More pangs will, schooled at forepangs, wilder wring.
Comforter, where, where is your comforting?
Mary, mother of us, where is your relief?
My cries heave, herds-long; huddle in a main, a chief
Woe, world-sorrow; on an age-old anvil wince and sing –
Then lull, then leave off. Fury had shrieked 'No ling-
ering! Let me be fell: force I must be brief'.

  O the mind, mind has mountains; cliffs of fall
Frightful, sheer, no-man-fathomed. Hold them cheap
May who ne'er hung there. Nor does long our small
Durance deal with that steep or deep. Here! creep,
Wretch, under a comfort serves in a whirlwind: all
Life death does end and each day dies with sleep.

Pitched Combines pitched in the sense of
'hurled' and also its musical sense.
Schooled at forepangs Taught by previous
experiences of grief.
Comforter See John 14, where the Holy Spirit
is called the Comforter.
Force Perforce.
Durance Combines 'endurance' and durance
as in 'durance vile'.
Fell Ruthless.

Justus quidem tu es, Domine

si disputem tecum: verumtamen justa loquar ad te:
Quare via impiorum prosperatur? &c.

Thou art indeed just, Lord, if I contend
With thee; but, sir, so what I plead is just.
Why do sinners' ways prosper? and why must
Disappointment all I endeavour end?

  Wert thou my enemy, O thou my friend,
How wouldst thou worse, I wonder, than thou dost
Defeat, thwart me? Oh, the sots and thralls of lust
Do in spare hours more thrive than I that spend,
Sir, life upon thy cause. See, banks and brakes
Now leavèd how thick! lacèd they are again
With fretty chervil, look, and fresh wind shakes
Them; birds build – but not I build; no, but strain,
Time's eunuch, and not breed one work that wakes.
Mine, O thou lord of life, send my roots rain.

The Latin title is from the Bible, Jeremiah 12:1: 'Righteous art thou, O LORD, when I plead with thee: yet let me talk with thee of thy judgments: Wherefore doth the way of the wicked prosper?' (Authorised Version). There are other references to the chapter in the poem, hence the '&c' in the title.
Sot   Drunkard.

Thrall   Slave, though with the added meaning of 'enthralled by'.
Brakes   Thickets.
Fretty chervil   Cow Parsley (see photograph overleaf).

Opposite: tree growing out of abandoned tank. Army ranges, Bordon, Hampshire

Two Kinds of Despair: 'No worst' and 'Justus quidem'

The desolate grief and Ecclesiastes-like resignation of 'No worst' does not represent Hopkins's final position in the 'terrible sonnets'. 'No worst' concludes with the fatalistic (and for a Christian believer, not very comforting) pronouncement that death brings life to an end and sleep brings each day to a close. The sonnet is an angry cry of pain. In 'Justus quidem ...', the poet sees his argument through to the end.

The passage from the Book of Jeremiah to which the title refers is the story of the prophet's dramatic confrontation with God, in which he demands why it is that the wicked do so well when those who are God's people suffer so much. He was neither the first nor the last to ask God that question, or to have the security of faith to interrogate God directly and demandingly. St Teresa of Avila hurled the same accusation at God: 'It is no wonder you have so many enemies, when one sees how badly you treat your friends.' Then, said Asaph in Psalm 73, 'I went into the sanctuary of God; then understood I their end.'

Nor was Jeremiah the first or last to find that his question received no direct answer from God; and that what had seemed a disputation was in fact shouting into a silent void.

The courtroom atmosphere of the Latin quotation is maintained by the structure of the poem; no experimental form but a conventional sonnet. (Hopkins said that it was to be read slowly, *molto adagio*.) Within this controlled poem, however, there are angry questions, just as Jeremiah's anger burned against God. Three questions are put. One, Why do sinners prosper? Two, Why does everything that he, Hopkins, tries to do end in failure? Three, Would it make much practical difference if God were his enemy rather than his friend?

The genius of the poem is the universalising of the poet's private grief so that the reader is not simply eavesdropping on a private wrangle but is forced to consider large, even cosmic issues. Hopkins achieves this by referring outside his immediate situation to the happy situation of the cow parsley and the loveliness of spring. Everything grows and flourishes, but the poet, by comparison with fecund nature, breeds 'not one work that wakes'. The reference to nature is carried over to the moving last line, where humble piety and simple faith indicate that Hopkins has not been overwhelmed by his own arguments.

Cow Parsley ('Fretty chervil')

150

Breaks and Diversions

The years in Dublin, which Hopkins was to call 'wasted years', were years of hard work, depression and poor health, but there were breaks in the clouds; his friendship with Coventry Patmore was growing, he was in good touch with Robert Bridges (whose medical training made him sometimes quite seriously worried about the state of Hopkins's health) and with R. W. Dixon; and there were stimulating friends such as Kate Tynan, a very modern 20-year-old who shared a liking for Patmore's poetry, and wrote poetry herself. At Dublin, too, his previous intermittent interest in music flourished. Ireland was a country full of music, and Hopkins gained much satisfaction from developing what seems to have been a small but significant talent in that art.

One friend he made outside the university was Miss Cassidy, an elderly, kindly spinster who lived in the town of Monasterevan, about thirty miles from Dublin. Hopkins spent many holidays at her house, a spacious property surrounded by greenery. At Monasterevan he found his imagination kindled; several poems had their first impulse there. Gradually he moved on from the despair of the 'terrible sonnets'. Moments of happiness broke the abiding pessimism that threatened often to engulf him: the sense that he had squandered his gifts, that he was a failure in his vocation, that he had not pushed himself hard enough in his service to God. And among the contraries of the religious life, deep certainties rooted inside him began to find a voice again in his poems, as in 'That Nature is a Heraclitean Fire' (p. 161).

His university duties permitted a good allowance of holidays. He did not spend them all at Monasterevan, but took the opportunity to explore other parts of Ireland as well. The remaining poems in this book were written during such holidays: 'Harry Ploughman' in Dromore in Northern Ireland, and 'That Nature is a Heraclitean Fire' on a day's holiday in the middle of the examination season. There is plenty of innovation and experimentation in these later poems: one that he wrote on unemployment, 'Tom's Garland', even baffled Bridges and compelled Hopkins to concede that the particular innovative style he had chosen for that poem was a blind alley.

Miss Cassidy's house, Monasterevan

152

Harry Ploughman

The manuscript of 'Harry Ploughman' in Hopkins's handwriting, with metrical annotations

Harry Ploughman

Hard as hurdle arms, with a broth of goldish flue
Breathed round; the rack of ribs; the scooped flank; lank
Rope-over thigh; knee-nave; and barrelled shank –
    Head and foot, shoulder and shank –
By a grey eye's heed steered well, one crew, fall to;
Stand at stress. Each limb's barrowy brawn, his thew
That onewhere curded, onewhere sucked or sank –
    Soared or sank –,
Though as a beechbole firm, finds his, as at a roll-call, rank
And features, in flesh, what deed he each must do –
    His sinew-service where do.

He leans to it, Harry bends, look. Back, elbow, and liquid waist
In him, all quail to the wallowing o' the plough: 's cheek crimsons;
    curls
Wag or crossbridle, in a wind lifted, windlaced –
    See his wind-lilylocks-laced;
Churlsgrace, too, child of Amansstrength, how it hangs or hurls
Them – broad in bluff hide his frowning feet lashed! raced
With, along them, cragiron under and cold furls –
    With-a-fountain's shining-shot furls.

Hurdle A screen made of woven branches.
Flue Down or wool; Hopkins uses it for 'hair'.
Rack Evokes culinary images of beef.
Thew Strength.
Curded Bulged.
Churlsgrace The grace of a peasant or 'churl'.

Frowning A typical Hopkins obscurity that allows several interpretations, all adding to the meaning. Suggestions have included 'advancing aggressively' and the wrinkles in Harry's boots. Perhaps there is an echo of 'froward' too – an impetuous, perhaps too impetuous, urge to press ahead.

Sinew-Service
Harry Ploughman

This poem has more in common with 'Felix Randal' than the fact that both poems happen to have men's names as their titles. Harry the Ploughman is what Felix was in his prime; the whole poem glorifies the physical beauty and power of this labourer, just as Hopkins does the wasted strength of Felix in the closing exuberant lines of the earlier sonnet.

The text is rather dense, and the vocabulary sometimes obscure; only a few footnotes have been provided here, because the effect of the poem is enhanced by not pinning down every word to a precise meaning. The text has a compelling visual quality as if we are watching a portrait painter add more and more details, each acutely observed and all characteristic of the man. 'The scooped flank', for example, accurately records the muscle shape of a thigh tensed in exertion.

There is no profound meaning or message to this poem; it is a celebration of strength written by one who often lacked it. Hopkins called it 'a direct vision of a ploughman, without afterthought', and envisaged it being performed as a stage recitation, with a chorus supplying the refrain.

The major success of the poem as literary style is the skilful passage to the second section, where having painted a picture of a massive and strong man in the first section, Hopkins proceeds to set him into motion. 'He leans to it, Harry bends, look.' Movement irrupts into the poem; the liquid movement of Harry's muscled body, the evocative 'wallowing' of the plough. The effect is curiously satisfying; even the poet's helpful prompts ('Harry bends, look ...), inescapable as they are, heighten rather than dampen the imaginative experience.

Triumph over Tribulations

The poems that end this selection are not from the Sonnets of Desolation, the 'terrible sonnets', but from the poems that Hopkins wrote at the end of his life, when the certainties of faith were underpinning the poems so strongly that, when one looks back at the terrible sonnets, it is hard to imagine the state of mind that produced the very real despair they reflect.

One aspect of the story has recently been explored afresh and casts considerable light on various aspects of Hopkins's work. What precisely was the physical ailment that recurred throughout his life, spoiling his enthusiasm for new challenges, creating despondency when zest was needed, and causing him chronic and recurrent pain? Whatever it was, it even interfered with the proper observances of the Jesuit year, for his superiors forbade him to undertake Lenten fasts, on health grounds.

In 1997 Kenneth Flegel, a Canadian doctor, examined the Hopkins literature and tried to answer the question of why Gerard Manley Hopkins died so young and why so many doctors were unable to cure him of his various complaints. By analysing the pattern of the disease and the symptoms recorded by Hopkins and others (Robert Bridges, for example, wrote many letters of concern over Hopkins's health), and noting factors such as the very long period of ill health that preceded his death, and the recurrent eye trouble of which he complained, Dr Flegel concluded that the likeliest diagnosis was Crohn's disease rather than typhoid fever, the cause of death usually suggested (typhoid was rampant in Ireland at the time of Hopkins's death). Dr Flegel's comment is, in the circumstances, deeply moving:

> Hopkins's life seems to have been one of obedience, drudgery and indifferent health. His poetry, especially when read aloud, speaks of an inner life that triumphed over the tribulations. (*The Lancet*, Vol. 349, 5 April 1997, p. 1017)

Newman House lies to the south of
St Stephen's Green. Today, as in Hopkins's time,
the Green is a tranquil haven from the bustle of the city

That Nature is a Heraclitean Fire and of the comfort of the Resurrection

Cloud-puffball, torn tufts, tossed pillows | flaunt forth, then chevy on an air-
built thoroughfare: heaven-roysterers, in gay-gangs | they throng;
   they glitter in marches.
Down roughcast, down dazzling whitewash, | wherever an elm arches,
Shivelights and shadowtackle in long | lashes lace, lance, and pair.
Delightfully the bright wind boisterous | ropes, wrestles, beats earth bare
Of yestertempest's creases; in pool and rut peel parches
Squandering ooze to squeezed | dough, crust, dust; stanches, starches
Squadroned masks and manmarks | treadmire toil there
Footfretted in it. Million-fuelèd, | nature's bonfire burns on.
But quench her bonniest, dearest | to her, her clearest-selvèd spark
Man, how fast his firedint, | his mark on mind, is gone!
Both are in an unfathomable, all is in an enormous dark
Drowned. O pity and indig | nation! Manshape, that shone
Sheer off, disseveral, a star, | death blots black out; nor mark
    Is any of him at all so stark
But vastness blurs and time | beats level. Enough! the Resurrection,
A heart's-clarion! Away grief's gasping, | joyless days, dejection.
    Across my foundering deck shone
A beacon, an eternal beam. | Flesh fade, and mortal trash
Fall to the residuary worm; | world's wildfire, leave but ash:
    In a flash, at a trumpet crash,
I am all at once what Christ is, | since he was what I am, and
This Jack, joke, poor potsherd, | patch, matchwood, immortal diamond,
    Is immortal diamond.

Cloud-puffball Air and water are the most unstable of all the elements.
Tossed pillows Clouds.
Chevy Scamper.
Gay-gangs A reference to Walt Whitman.
Shivelights Shivers (splinters) of light.
Masks Impressions, as in death masks etc.

Bonfire Hopkins has funeral pyres in mind.
Firedint A Hopkins word meaning the impress of fire upon human beings.
Disseveral Hopkins is combining 'disseveral' and 'several'.
Patch Fool.

Immortal Diamond
The Comfort of the Resurrection

'That Nature is a Heraclitean Fire' is a poem that needs some additional information if one is to get more from it than Hopkins's sheer delight in words (which in this poem is considerable!).

The poem at first glance looks extremely complex, but as we have seen throughout this book, a good first step is to read it aloud. To help to keep the correct balance of stresses in the line, the 'caesura' or breaks have been indicated by vertical bars, giving the poem something of the look of a page from a psalter. But the gravity of liturgy is very far from the exuberance of this poem, that begins with words and images flying in all directions as the poet brilliantly evokes the flux and fire into which, the philosopher Heraclitus taught, all things must ultimately resolve.

Technically the form of the poem is a 'long' sonnet, but a good reading of it, either on the page or aloud, is unlikely to be distracted by technical matters. The poem contains two energetic concepts, the juxtaposition of which creates its enormous energy.

The key that unlocks Hopkins's meaning is that he is comparing two things. One is the ancient belief described by Heraclitus in the sixth century BC, that the most important element is fire. All other things only have individual identity insofar as, by ceaseless activity and strife, they separate themselves from the fire. So nothing endures, nothing is ever completely at rest, everything is in a constant state of motion. The poem is full of images of insubstantiality ('Cloud-puffball', 'death blots black out', etc.) and of ceaseless motion ('glitter in marches', 'bright wind boisterous', etc.)

Against this, with the energy of profound refusal ('Enough! the Resurrection'), Hopkins shows us the biblical teaching that human beings, 'Jack' (= Everyman), are immortal, the 'diamond' that is the purest product of fire; the ceaseless turmoil of the fallen world will not destroy us but will result in our purification. As 'poor potsherd' we are the broken pots in the potter's workshop, but we are (cf. Isaiah 64:8) the work of God's hand. Lights penetrate this dark world, like 'shadowtackle' (the trees outlined against the sky like ships' rigging) and 'whitewash' (rain on arching elm trees).

The poem resolves itself in the teaching of St Paul: this mortal will put on immortality. Though to human eye 'Manshape' is a star that 'death blots black out', yet there will come a resurrection, 'in a flash, at a trumpet crash' when the believer will become 'all at once what Christ is, since he was what I am'.

Stone cross in the grounds of St Beuno's

162

'Things might change ...'

The poems 'Justus quidem tu es' and 'That Nature is a Heraclitean Fire' were written within a short time of each other, which perhaps accurately reflects the state of Hopkins's mind in his final years. He lived at a time when death was an ever-present reality, and he found it particularly hard to bear when contemporaries died. In recent years his school friend Marcus Clarke had died in Australia, and his Oxford friend Martin Geldart, who had included a gentle caricature of Hopkins in his novel A Son of Belial, had been drowned. In these years too his friend William Addis left the Roman Catholic Church, which was a severe blow to him.

The labour of setting and marking examinations and the other duties of the academic life had proved as wearisome as Hopkins had feared they would, and holidays and other diversions failed to lift the burden entirely. He took some holidays away from Ireland but found himself too tired, after the exertions of teaching, properly to enjoy them. Physical problems continued to afflict him including rheumatism and the recurrence of eye trouble, leading eventually to spectacles being prescribed. But he tried to pick up old interests. He spent some time drawing again, and he attended concerts in Dublin and wrote some music of his own.

He experienced frustration in his writing; sometimes he began poems but could not complete them, a critical piece was accepted by a scholarly journal but apparently not published, another was accepted, foundered in much rewriting and was also not published.

Yet he was able in his stronger moments to take an objective view of his problems and disappointments. He saw his burden of work, his tiredness, his frustrations as all aspects of the same thing; crosses to be born, penances to strengthen his faith. In his stronger moments he saw even his trials as further spiritual growth. And he retained a basic optimism: 'I do not despair, things might change,' he wrote, but confessed his hopes were not high.

At various times in his life Hopkins tried his hand at writing music and also copied out others' compositions to study

164

165

The End

Early in the last twelve months of Hopkins's life, in August 1888, he went on holiday to Scotland with one of the professors from University College. Both men were in poor health and neither benefited much from the fresh air and exercise. Hopkins spent much of the time reading an adventure novel, *Two Years Before the Mast*, bringing to the yarn of naval life a critical literary eye.

Back in Dublin the duties of a new academic year's duties had to be faced and examinations prepared. He found it all excessively draining. His eyes were constantly sore, and he was not yet used to the spectacles that had been prescribed.

The poems of the final months were varied. He completed a patriotic piece, 'What shall I do for the land that bred me?', but such thoughts must only have heightened his sense of isolation that we have already seen in his poem 'To seem the stranger'. In October he was writing a sonnet in commemoration of the newly canonised St Alphonsus Rodriguez. By March 1889 he had reached the firmer ground of 'Justus quidem tu es', and in April he wrote 'The Shepherd's Brow,' which draws in part upon musical imagery to explore what seems to be in part a concept of Christ. His last poem (according to its date) was a sonnet addressed 'To R. B.'. It is an eloquent, thoughtful explanation of his recent poetic silence; in this 'winter world', inspiration comes rarely and with little rapture.

His final illness began gradually and lasted for six weeks. From its onset, Hopkins appears to have suspected that he would die from it. He made some final arrangements and requests, among them a strong hint to Robert Bridges that he would like his poems to be published after his death. By late May his health had declined to the point where his doctors formally warned him of the gravity of his illness, and his parents were sent for. Hopkins, who was lucid and aware of his surroundings, was distressed to think that his parents would see him so ill, but the meeting was a happy one. They remained in Dublin as their son grew increasingly weak, and were with him when he received the last rites on 8 June and died a few hours later.

His poems were, as he had requested, sent to Robert Bridges, and as he had wished, they were eventually published. He was buried in the Jesuit plot in Dublin's Glasnevin Cemetery. He was forty-four years old.

'I am so happy, I am so happy.'
The last words of Gerard Manley Hopkins, Society of Jesus, 1844–1889

Further Reading

We have not attempted to make this list exhaustive, but have restricted ourselves to books that we have enjoyed and which have been useful resources as we created this book. If you only have the time to read one book from this list, it should be Eleanor Ruggles's biography of Hopkins!

Texts

Gardner, W. H. and N. H. MacKenzie (eds), *The Poems of Gerard Manley Hopkins* (Oxford University Press, 4th edn 1970). A standard text.

Gardner, W. H. (ed.), *Gerard Manley Hopkins: a Selection from his Poems and Prose* (Penguin, 1953). This selection from the Gardner & MacKenzie *Poems* plus representative prose is a very useful cross-section of Hopkin's work as a whole.

Phillips, Catherine (ed.), *Gerard Manley Hopkins: Selected Poetry* (Oxford University Press, World's Classics, 1995/6). This is a comprehensive selection with good notes.

Thornton, R. K. R., *All My Eyes See: The Visual World of Gerard Manley Hopkins* (Ceolrith Press, 1975). This superb book, based on an exhibition, brings together drawings and other art by Hopkins and his family, together with photographs of Hopkins sites and other material. But the book goes much further than being merely a catalogue and discusses Hopkins's artistic work and its influence on his poetry. Profusely illustrated.

Van de Weyer, Robert (ed.), *The Complete Poems With Selected Prose: Gerard Manley Hopkins* (HarperCollins Fount, 1996). Very far from complete, in fact, but a selection of the most important poems.

Biographies and Studies

MacKenzie, Catherine, *York Notes on Selected Poems: Gerard Manley Hopkins* (Longmans Literature Guides, 1983). This 'exam crib' booklet makes a very thorough companion to getting to grips with Hopkins's poems for any reader.

Pick, John, *Gerard Manley Hopkins: Priest and Poet* (Oxford, 2nd edn 1966). Especially helpful in explaining the Catholic theology and Jesuit background to Hopkins's writings.

Ruggles, Eleanor, *Gerard Manley Hopkins: a Life* (John Lane the Bodley Head, 1947). A classic study. Ruggles is especially good at relating Hopkins to his times and at making connections that, while not always immediately obvious, profoundly increase understanding and enjoyment. Like Jones on Balliol (below), this is a book that is of absorbing interest almost irrespective of its subject.

Smith, Margaret D, *Holy Struggle: Unspoken Thought of Hopkins*, with photographs by Luci Shaw (Harold Shaw Publishers, USA, 1992). Hopkins's poetry and aspects of his life illuminated by sonnets by Margaret Smith.

Storey, Graham, *A Preface to Hopkins* (Longman, 2nd edn 1992). A very useful handbook with essays on a number of different aspects and detailed notes on the texts.

Watson, J. R., *The Poetry of Gerard Manley Hopkins* (Penguin Critical Studies, 1989). Watson is particularly helpful on Hopkins's poetic diction.

Historical Background

Butler, Perry (ed.), *Pusey Rediscovered* (SPCK, 1983). A revaluation published on the 150th anniversary of the Oxford Movement.

Chadwick, Owen, *The Victorian Church*, 2 vols (SCM, 1987). A magisterial study that superbly handles the cross-currents of English church life during Hopkins's lifetime.

Edwards, Paul, *Canute's Tower, St Beuno's* (Fowler Wright, 1990). Contains much useful information on the Jesuits as well as on St Beuno's itself.

Hinde, Thomas, *Highgate School: A History* (James and James, 1993).

Jones, John, *Balliol College: A History* (Oxford University Press, 2nd edn 1997).

Ker, Ian, *Newman and Conversion* (T & T Clark, 1997). Papers from an Oxford conference to mark the 150th anniversary of Newman's conversion to Roman Catholicism.

Sykes, Stephen and John Booty (eds), *The Study of Anglicanism* (SPCK, 1988). The historical chapter by Perry Butler (see above) is especially useful.

Vidler, Alec R., *The Church in an Age of Revolution: 1789 to the Present Day* (Penguin, rev. 1990). This volume in Penguin's very readable *History of the Church* is a good shorter alternative to Chadwick.

Other Resources

The Gerard Manley Hopkins Society, Monasterevin, Co. Kildare, Ireland
(NB that there are two spellings of Monasterevin; we have used the older
'Monasterevan' in our text.)

  The society aims to promote, celebrate and foster the works of Gerard Manley
Hopkins. It organises an annual Summer School and festival. Details of this and
membership may be obtained from: Richard O'Rourke, Gerard Manley Hopkins
Society, Monasterevin, Co. Kildare, Ireland.

E-mail: hopkins@iol.ie

The Gerard Manley Hopkins Resource Page on the Internet (World Wide
Web), created and maintained by David Jerome Callon, is a comprehensive listing
of Hopkins resources including archives, reviews, books, journals and much more.

http://www.creighton.edu/~dcallon/gmhpage.html

The Hopkins Quarterly is the only printed journal dealing specifically with Hopkins and his circle. The editor is Joseph J. Feeney S.J., Dept of English, St Jospeh's
University, Philadelphia PA 19131, USA.

E-mail: jfeeney@sju.edu

The Texts

We have used Robert Bridge's edition of 1918 as our basic text for the poems, preserving his sometimes rather idiosyncratic indentation but with a few minor changes for clarity.

Unreferenced quotations by Hopkins are taken from his published Notebooks, Letters and Journals, where they can be located easily by date.

We are glad to acknowledge with thanks the use of illustrative material from Campion House and Highgate School.

About Tricia and David Porter

Tricia Porter

Tricia Porter studied pharmacy at London University but went on to become a freelance photographer; one of her early projects was a documentary exhibition about community life in Bedford Street, in central Liverpool. The writer on that project was David Porter. Later they married.

Tricia's work has been featured in exhibitions, books, periodicals and television, and is in private collection in Britain, America and Europe. Her major exhibitions have included group exhibitions (by women photographers at the National Film Theatre, and a three-photographer exhibition at the Free University, Amsterdam), and solo exhibitions in many galleries on subject as diverse as tree studies, inner-city kids, village life in Selborne, and derelict army equipment on moorland ranges.

As a Community Arts worker, Tricia teaches photography to groups with special needs, and has organised a number of exhibitions in public galleries of work by groups such as people with learning disabilities and long-term prisoners.

In 1983 Tricia and David published *Through the Eyes of a Child* in which poems and text accompanied photographic studies of children.

David Porter

David Porter has qualifications in librarianship and degree in English literature. Since 1980 he has worked as a full-time writer and editor. His published books include four volumes of poetry, two plays and a novel, *The Vienna Passage*, which reflects a life-long love of music. He has contributed articles to several reference works including *The Oxford Companion to Twentieth-Century Literature in English*. His other books include the authorised biography of Laszlo Tokes the instigator of the Romanian revolution, a biography of Mother Teresa and a book of conversations with Malcolm Muggeridge. He has written extensively on the media and on children's play, and has lectured on a wide range of subjects in venues as diverse as Budapest University and the Islamic Academy, Cambridge (where he delivered a paper on Barbie dolls).

vledgements

is not acknowledged below are the
sion to reproduce the photographs
› the pubishers.

Index of Names and Titles